Challenging the DALEY MACHINE

For Marian

Contents

Foreword

MIKE ROYKO

SOMEBODY suggested that I introduce an alderman.

That suited me fine, because I am always happy to introduce an alderman anytime I can catch one and a grand jury is in session.

I've always enjoyed Chicago's aldermen, and I believe that if they went away the city would be a much poorer place for their absence. Just how much poorer I didn't know, because it would depend on how much you can stuff in a suitcase.

I wanted to introduce Claude W. B. Holman, because he can hit high C when he is in the mood, and I wanted to see how many glasses would break. They said they didn't think he would be here, so I asked about Alderman Fred Roti from the First Ward. I am not sure what he can hit or break, and I am not sure I want to find out.

But they said I should introduce Alderman Leon Despres. We had an argument because I didn't believe Despres really was an alderman. If he is an alderman, how come he rides around his ward on a bicycle instead of in a Cadillac? But they said he is going to get a tandem and have somebody do the pedaling.

So I'm introducing Alderman Despres. Throughout his career he has been in the forefront of just about every decent, worthwhile effort made to improve life in this city. Being in the forefront, he is usually the first to be hit on the head with the mayor's gavel. Some of my

---

This was Mike Royko's introduction of Alderman Despres as a speaker at a meeting for State Representative Robert E. Mann in Hyde Park on January 30, 1972.

enjoyable afternoons have been spent listening to the rhythmic beat of gavel and head, with Claude Holman singing an aria.

I will try to touch on some of Len's lesser-known accomplishments.

Len was first elected to the city council in 1955. That was also the year I got my first job as a reporter. And that was the same year Mayor Daley was elected to his first term. Yet he takes all the credit for those glory years. And you don't read any articles about Len Despres in *Town and Country*.

In 1965, Len became the first alderman during the Daley administration to have the city council's sergeant-at-arms sicced on him because he wouldn't sit down. Until that time the mayor had never had an alderman defy him when he said, "Sit." In fact most of them not only sit, they bark and roll over.

In 1968 when the mayor said, "Shoot to kill," Despres single-handedly started panic in city hall by saying the mayor had "lost his equilibrium." Shouting "What does it look like?" thousands of pay-rollers launched a search for it. So far it's still missing.

Len is believed to be the only alderman who can speak five languages. But no matter which one he uses, his associates don't understand him.

He was responsible for a major public works project when they had to make a special incinerator just for his resolutions and ordinances.

And finally he's the only member of the present city council to have been shot while holding office. Others are far more deserving of that distinction.

Preface

KENAN HEISE

*Chicago has also produced outstanding reformers like Jane Addams,
Edward Dunne, Saul Alinsky, Clarence Darrow, Charles Merriam,
and Paul Douglas. This is the tradition from which Leon Despres
comes. Fighting Machine politics, racism, and corruption strengthens
any man or woman. It did Despres.*
Former alderman Dick Simpson, *Chicago Journal*, August 8, 2002

IN HIS memoirs, Leon Despres tells his story of the political wars
fought in Chicago while he was alderman of the Fifth Ward from
1955 to 1975. Nationally, these decades represented an era of dramatic
change. They became deeply marked with a growing sensitivity to
the civil and human rights of people long denied equal opportunity
in seeking the American dream. Chicago—although not the South,
where major battles took place—was a place where the struggle ensued
and victories were achieved.

Alderman Despres played a key role. His words and stifled protests
refused to let the city write off the poor and the victims of discrimination. His actions and message were directed toward forging a new
Chicago, one molded by even-handed justice and fashioned by a
relentless concern for the human needs of all its residents. Although
usually defeated in Mayor Richard J. Daley's city council, his proposed
ordinances and resolutions served as the guide and pattern for what
was to be. Most of his fellow aldermen considered him ill suited for
such an epic role. In a city government run on clout and patronage,

he had neither. In a city council where boodle was a tradition, he irritated many of his fellow members by being incorruptible.

During council proceedings, Alderman Despres's microphone was often turned off by the mayor when he spoke. Selected aldermen regularly interrupted by calling for a "point of order." Mayor Richard J. Daley then used each such request as a parliamentary tactic to take the floor away from him. Still, the Fifth Ward alderman created and methodically presented to Chicago policies and solutions that eventually won the day. Sometimes, mere months after he witnessed the defeat of ordinances he had proposed, he saw them resubmitted by other aldermen using slightly different language. They were then passed. Other times, this was done years and even decades later. On occasion, sponsors righteously, but not rightly, proclaimed that their proposals were not connected in any way to his earlier ones. Newspaper writers often viewed such statements with cynicism.

Alderman Despres was the individual who both figuratively and literally stood up for Chicago during those years. Film clips from the era show a vital man with a determined face quietly pulling himself up to his full stature to drive home his point or make his objection. He was, above all, persistent. He chose never to disdain a city he found imperfect but rather to embrace and attempt to improve it. Hundreds of times, if not thousands, he arose from his seat in the Chicago City Council to speak out, protest what was wrong for the city, praise what was right, and offer ordinances and resolutions to do something specific and lasting about it.

In his aldermanic role, Leon Despres worked diligently to establish an active record not only in the council proceedings but also in the media. He listened attentively to his constituents and gladly addressed small and large groups throughout Chicago willing to hear his words. Above all, he used his seat to get his message across quickly and succinctly. He confronted racial segregation, the lead-paint poisoning of the city's small children, destruction of the city's great architecture, denial of employment opportunity for women, and the stranglehold of patronage on the city. Speaking of residential segregation, he insisted that it was "the single most important factor hampering Chicago's development as a great city."

The people of the Fifth Ward, who had elected him their representative, reelected him four times until he chose not to run again. A fellow independent alderman, William Cousins, said of him in a *Hyde Park Herald* article at the time of Leon's retirement: "He has a great sensitivity to human needs and is a person with the utmost concern for the protection of civil rights of all persons. He spoke particularly for those who are at the greatest disadvantage and who have suffered the greatest deprivation."

Challenging the Daley Machine: A Chicago Alderman's Memoir proclaims an unwavering belief in democracy and its potential in an urban setting. The future, says Leon Despres, can and must belong equally to each man, woman, and child. Never, he says, should income, color, gender, or disability become bars over which people are required to jump in order to claim their right to life, liberty, and the pursuit of happiness.

In the twenty-first century, the call to arms against political oppression, corruption, and disregard for the rights and needs of individuals continues to be as necessary as the fight against all other attacks on this nation's democracy.

Acknowledgments

MERVIN BLOCK, master of communication in the English language, read the entire transcript and awarded it his disapproval. From him, disapproval is almost equal to high praise. It means "pretty good and could be worse." He signaled many but not all of my awkwardnesses. For instance, where I wrote, "Many victories were won," his wry note was "Did you ever hear of a victory that wasn't won?"

Victoria Haas typed the entire manuscript over and over. With her magic, she transformed multiple handwritings, tapes, and rough typescripts into smooth, orderly, beautiful pages.

Judy Royko and publisher Bruce Sagan gave permission to print Mike Royko's joyful 1972 introduction of me as a speaker.

Without Kenan Heise, this book would not have been written. He has been the Engine, the Yahoo, the propulsion that brought this work out of the depths to a visible screen. The writing is mine, but he is the one who kept me writing. His vast book publishing experience, his years of professional writing, his devotion to the subject, his judgment, his wide knowledge, and his friendship kept me going when nothing else could.

Challenging the DALEY MACHINE

The Precinct Captains Celebrate Richard J. Daley's Election

1

Chicago ain't ready for a reform mayor.
Alderman Mathias "Paddy" Bauler, April 5, 1955

It was election day, April 5, 1955.

In a former tavern turned Forty-third Ward headquarters at 409 West North Avenue, just west of Sedgwick Street, Democratic precinct captains were celebrating. They were gloating over the defeat of Robert E. Merriam, the Republican and reform candidate for mayor.

The ward's Democratic committeeman, Alderman Mathias "Paddy" Bauler, the boss of the precinct captains gathered in the room, made his famous pronouncement to *Chicago Tribune* city hall reporter Edward Schreiber.

"Chicago ain't ready for a reform mayor," he said.

Schreiber later personally acknowledged to me that he had changed the quotation to "Chicago ain't ready for reform."

Although it had been a tough campaign, almost from the beginning there was little doubt about the outcome. The regular organization, the Cook County Democratic Party, had so many precinct workers—public employees whose job was to bring in the votes for the dominant party—that they swamped the opposition. The citywide margin of victory for Daley was 126,967 votes out of 1.3 million cast.

The Democratic Machine that ran Chicago and local government comprised eighty committeemen, one representing each of the fifty

3

city wards and thirty townships outside the city. Each of them dispensed city jobs and headed a local patronage army whose purpose was to win elections. On this day, they had succeeded in putting in office one of their own.

Mayor Martin J. Kennelly, although a Democrat like them, had been systemically reducing the number of "temps," that is, city employees not covered by civil service. The new committeeman-mayor had pledged to increase that number and to appoint a lot of non–civil service employees. He had made alliances with other committeemen, especially William Dawson, who served as leader of the black committeemen. They and Daley had an understanding that Daley would not interfere with patronage appointments, illegal South Side "policy" (or number racket) lottery games, unlicensed South Side jitney cabs, and other similar sources of their under-the-table revenue.

One significant holdout from the Daley alliance had been Frank Keenan, the Forty-eighth Ward committeeman. He had voted against giving Eleventh Democratic Ward committeeman Daley the party endorsement and then had served in the Democratic primary as campaign chairman for Kennelly.

And on that day, April 5, 1955, I was voted into my first term in the city council as an independent, the representative for the people of the Fifth Ward. The Fifth Ward then was the area abutting Lake Michigan for two miles from 5100 to 6700 south. It included all of the Hyde Park community (5100 to 5900 south as far west as Cottage Grove Avenue) and half of the Woodlawn community as far south as Sixty-fifth Street. Of about sixty thousand constituents, 60 percent were white and 40 percent African American.

Chicago did not present a pretty picture to a new alderman, but it did offer an opportunity for challenge. The city for which I now shared political responsibility cried out for equal opportunity, especially for blacks and women.

Chicago had become a place where clout and bribes (sometimes called campaign contributions) were the lubricant for city services and political favors.

The federal government, for its part, later indicted, convicted, and imprisoned more than twenty Chicago aldermen.

There was no overall city plan.

Housing segregation was unconstrained.

The criminal Mafia was in tight control of at least two inner-city wards.

There was so much to be done on April 5, 1955.

An Accidental Alderman Is Elected

2

. . . a stunning 3,700 vote victory.
Hyde Park Herald, April 6, 1955

MY POLITICAL career was thrust upon me. I am thankful it was.

It began one Saturday morning in early November 1954, in the Hyde Park office of Chicago's Fifth Ward alderman, Robert Merriam. On the previous Tuesday, a general election had just resulted in major Democratic victories. Merriam himself was preparing to become the Republican candidate for mayor of Chicago in the April 1955 election. On that 1954 Saturday, he had invited Louis Silverman, a public relations professional; Robert Picken, a candy manufacturer; Richard Meyer, a clothing retailer; and me, a lawyer, to find a strong candidate for alderman to succeed and support him.

Merriam, until then an independent Democrat, had obtained Republican Party support for mayor. To win the election, he was confronted with the might of the thousands of precinct workers in the Democratic Party Machine. In a Democratic city, he would need to gather all the liberal, independent, and Democratic votes possible. County Clerk Richard J. Daley, who in 1953 had become chairman of the Democratic Party of Cook County, was his party's candidate for mayor. By law, Illinois required aldermanic candidates to run without party labels. As we talked on that November Saturday, I had no reason to think I might be the candidate, much less become the elected alderman. Why did Merriam turn to us? We were officers of the Independent Voters of Illinois, which had a ten-year record of public support for liberal and honorable candidates. Moreover, we had started doing something new. Instead of limiting our electoral work to endorsing candidates, printing sample ballots, and relying on public appeals, IVI had begun to canvass for candidates whom we ourselves had chosen. The difference between IVI's precinct canvassing and the Machine's was that the Machine could field an army of patronage employees, while IVI had to recruit energetic volunteers.

Our first new-style campaign had been run in 1953, when we jumped into a special aldermanic election in the Twenty-fifth Ward on the Near West Side. We had chosen Fred Hilbruner to run against a dictatorial committeeman, Vito Marzullo. Marzullo induced a pliant Election Commission to throw our candidate off the ballot for having "defective signatures" on the nominating petitions. Still, we got two thousand write-in votes (twelve hundred of which were counted.) We carried one precinct.

To Marzullo, a loss of even that one precinct had been a blow. For years afterward, when he and I conversed in the city council, he would often refer to it bitterly.

"Somebody lied to me," he would say.

He felt that his iron grip on the Twenty-fifth Ward had been affected and that, through malice or incompetence, his captain had failed to give him accurate advance information. As a capable Machine committeeman, he knew that before the election he was expected to give an accurate assessment of voter strength to the party chairman. Only then could the party know how to deploy troops.

When Daley was party chairman, he called in the ward committeemen before each election to give him their figures. He demanded accuracy. He was angry if a committeeman overstated the vote and just as upset if the committeeman understated it. Probably Marzullo was embarrassed because he had told Daley he would carry every precinct but did not do so.

Invigorated by our Twenty-fifth Ward campaign, we launched one for state representative in the Hyde Park–Woodlawn district for the April 1954 primary. Louis Silverman prevailed on Marmaduke Carter, a public school teacher, to run. The incumbent state representative was Louis Berman. Our slogan was "Get the hacks off our backs." When we announced the campaign, I received a startling telephone call from Jacob Arvey, the remarkably successful Twenty-fourth Ward West Side committeeman. He pleaded, "Why don't you let Berman have it?" It was our first intimation that we might someday succeed. We lost to Berman, but we got fifty-four hundred votes.

The IVI had supported Merriam enthusiastically in his aldermanic election campaigns in 1947 and 1951 as well as on reform issues he fought for in the city council. In 1954, of all the Fifth Ward support groups Merriam might have turned to for help, the IVI had the strongest philosophical affinity and, with our new electoral abilities, the greatest support that counted— precinct work.

Merriam had set a high standard on all aldermanic issues: governmental efficiency, housing, planning, crime, integration, honesty in campaign funds, attention to constituents, and effectiveness in communication. In 1947, the Fifth Ward Democratic committeeman, Barnet Hodes, had quarreled with the incumbent alderman, Bertram Moss, and had selected Merriam as a candidate who could add independent support. Merriam's father, Charles Merriam, had headed the University of Chicago's political science department and had been one of Chicago's greatest aldermen. In 1947 and 1951, "Merriam for alderman" resounded like the tones of the University of Chicago carillon.

In 1954, Alderman Merriam could have been reelected overwhelmingly; instead he decided to run for mayor, as his late father had done twice. Robert Merriam would have been a splendid mayor, and for just that reason, the Machine did not want him. There was no chance of his winning the Democratic primary. Consequently, he decided he would have to run as a Republican candidate against a handpicked Democratic candidate.

At our November 1954 meeting in Merriam's office, we agreed to perform what he asked—find a strong aldermanic candidate. In doing so we were thrilled to be creating an important election campaign and not just reacting to candidates sponsored by others. Politically, we felt we were coming of age. Realizing that the aldermanic fight would be a hard one, we determined to find a candidate who might win.

We went to work. The ward had eighty precincts. Each of them had an experienced Machine precinct captain and at least one assistant. The Democratic Party's ward headquarters had a full-time support staff. We, on the other hand, had no regular captain in any precinct. We had not one patronage worker. What we did have was enthusiasm and a Fifth Ward record of independent political support.

Earlier there had been brave Fifth Ward independent aldermanic campaigns against the Machine; brave but without victories. In 1935, the future alderman and U.S. senator Paul H. Douglas—then a University of Chicago professor of economics—had managed a gallant campaign (with local Republican support) for divinity professor Joseph Artman. I had managed an even more modest campaign for economics professor Maynard Krueger, a Socialist. In 1939, Paul Douglas himself ran and won with Machine support. He resigned in 1942 to join the Marines. In 1943, independent political science professor Walter Johnson ran and lost. In 1947, Robert Merriam won with Machine support; but, once in office, he flowered into independence.

At a 1954 Fifth Ward Democratic Party meeting, Committeeman Hodes announced that the Fifth Ward Democratic Organization had won every aldermanic election and predicted it always would. Neither his faithful audience nor almost anyone else in the ward had reason to doubt him.

In the quest for a strong candidate, IVI's Louis Silverman operated with political alchemy as he took executive charge. He had managed the IVI campaigns for Fred Hilbruner for Twenty-fifth Ward alderman in 1953 and for Marmaduke Carter for state representative in the 1954 primary.

Drawing up a list of "invincible" potential winners, we plunged into a search for a candidate. Silverman organized a community candidate search committee. One after another, however, our sure-thing candidates declined. Each one knew there would be a bruising political fight and believed it would be in vain.

We grew desperate. This might be our greatest chance to elect our own candidate, and yet we could not persuade any winning candidate to run. Then without my knowledge, Louis Silverman, Robert Picken, and Richard Meyer held a meeting of key IVI insiders.

"We're in a fix," I imagine they said. "We have the best opportunity ever for a great campaign and we can't get a decent candidate to run. We are really scraping the bottom of the barrel. The nominating petitions have to be circulated and filed in three weeks and time is running out. We need to start a petition drive right away. What about Despres? He's definitely not an establishment person, but maybe he has enough going for him. He's a Hyde Park homeowner, a family man, an IVI chairman, a University of Chicago graduate, a member of Reform Jewish Congregation KAM, has no scandals, has had lots of legal cases on civil liberties, discrimination, and labor, and he can talk all right. He's not what we've been looking for, but under the circumstances we could go with him. We haven't anyone else." Whatever their doubts, desperation won out.

In all my political activity, I had never considered myself a candidate. I believed my record was too radical. After asking the selection committee for Thanksgiving weekend to think it over, I talked to my wife, Marian, as well as a few friends and finally decided to do it. The campaign, I reasoned, would have three support bases—our own organization, the small Fifth Ward Republican organization committed to Merriam for mayor, and the enthusiastic independent support for Merriam. This was more than the IVI had ever put together in any campaign.

We believed we had a chance to win or, if not, at least to make a respectable showing and not just the six hundred votes Maynard Krueger had received in 1935. I had to switch gears. I had been a noncandidate; then I was a reluctant candidate; and very soon, I would become an energetic candidate.

The campaign quickly erupted. It created much more excitement than we had anticipated. Louis Silverman built a brilliant volunteer political organization. Richard Meyer and Robert Picken provided stability. Victor DeGrazia, Barbara O'Connor, and Abner Mikva brought invaluable insights. Political science professor Jerome Kerwin chaired the campaign. More and more people began to volunteer to work as precinct canvassers, office workers, fund-raisers, writers, drivers, publicists, and even sandwich makers. Although we had only one paid campaign organizer and never enough money, we outweighed our opposition in talent ten to one. The Machine ran George Uretz, a capable lawyer but an out-and-out Machine image, longtime precinct captain, and patronage appointee.

For the campaign, my life was probed in all its details. I had to appear before committees and compete with other candidates for support—the Citizens Search Committee, the Republican Party organization, Hyde Park groups, Woodlawn groups, and even, pro forma, the hostile Democratic Party organization, which had invited all candidates to submit their qualifications.

I spoke to every organization that was willing to listen to me. Workers put on coffee meetings, often three or four a day. I joined precinct workers in canvassing precincts. I presented myself to every pastor in the ward.

Bob Merriam advised: "See Larry Kimpton, the president of the University of Chicago, and see the president of the Hyde Park Bank." I did. These two men headed two groups—the university administration and the business community—which needed to be won over. Neither one made a commitment. Every Sunday morning, a growing campaign committee met at my home for coffee, rolls, support, and strategy. An inner group met informally and daily.

Political campaigning in Chicago was quite different then. Everything depended almost entirely on persistent precinct work. That is why the mercenary patronage armies were usually decisive, with the regular Democrats having many times more workers than their opponents. People responded freely then to the doorbell ringing of canvassers. There was not yet the pervasive fear of crime that kept doors closed. Our greatest precinct problem was in the high-rises and the apartment hotels, which often denied access to outside precinct workers. In them we would try to recruit a resident to act as canvasser.

Newspaper endorsements proved important. The Republican committeeman, John Leonard East, said the *Chicago Daily News* endorsement, which I received, was worth eight hundred votes in our ward. Local newspaper endorsements helped mightily. Expensive television could not be beamed to just a single ward. Radio exposure could be helpful if you could get it free as news. The local *Hyde Park Herald* was crucially important.

Possibility of victory depended on intensive and preferably repeated canvassing; identifying, persuading, and registering voters; mingling with voters; and then, on election day, organizing a huge effort to bring out all favorable voters, prevent illegal voting, and obtain an honest count. In a few precincts, especially where there were still paper ballots, the Democratic Machine captains were experts at fraud, misregistration, illegal voting, miscounting, misreporting, and—when advantageous—creating turmoil.

I tried to do my best. I was worried we lacked money or enough precinct canvassing. Also, we had some defections, and we grew discouraged when people did not carry out assignments. Fortunately, besides being constantly anxious, I was heartened by growing support and favorable indications.

As the campaign started, a sociologist, the father of our present state representative, Barbara Flynn Currie, told me, "Len, now you'll have to start being nice to everybody." It was not always easy. I shook thousands of hands on street corners, on train platforms, at bus stops, in shopping areas, and in meeting after meeting. John Leonard East said, "It's hard for people to vote against someone they have shaken hands with." He also recommended visiting barber shops, "where people talk."

My reception in the black precincts, which were mostly in Woodlawn, proved a revelation. With my long record on civil rights, I received a better personal reception and vote than any earlier white candidate had, but still we lost those precincts to the Democratic organization captains. In later elections, after I had proved myself in office, I would carry many of those precincts. In 1955, there was a deep skepticism, born of too many disappointments, from unproven white candidates promising justice. As a result, most of the black voters went with the precinct captain who did tangible favors.

Louis Silverman understood better than I that our hope in 1955 did not lie in winning those precincts but in doing so well in them that we would reduce the traditional Machine majority. In the election, the regular Democrats carried Woodlawn, but by far fewer votes than they had expected.

We had to go into a second round. In the February election, we were ahead of the Machine candidate by a thousand votes but lacked a clear majority. Two candidates were eliminated, Hugh Matchett, the conservative Republican, and Dorothy O'Brien Morgenstern, Mayor Kennelly's candidate. She had good support from voters connected to the University of Chicago. Just as Robert Merriam had sought a strong pro-Merriam candidate for alderman, Mayor Kennelly, hoping for renomination, found an attractive pro-Kennelly candidate. The two highest candidates, George Uretz and I, then went into a run-off. In the run-off most of the Matchett and Morgenstern supporters proved anti-Machine and voted for me.

After the personal exhaustion of the February campaign, I had to ask myself, "Do we possibly have to do all this again in April?" We did, and it was more exciting than the first time. Like racers who have won their initial heat, the campaign workers and I ran with renewed confidence and enthusiasm. Our majority was startling. We achieved what the *Hyde Park Herald* proclaimed "a stunning 3,700 vote victory."

In April 1955, we showed that at least in one ward it could be done. Afterward, we would see a chance to choose a winning candidate in the April 1956 state legislature primary election, and instead of a vain search, we would find candidates knocking at our door. The IVI would have to decide among University of Chicago professor Maynard Krueger, publisher Bruce Sagan, Roosevelt University professor George Watson, and a promising young lawyer named Abner Mikva. The IVI selected Mikva. Thus, the April 1955 election that sent the first independent alderman to the city council also opened the door to Abner Mikva's stellar political career.

My Beloved Hyde Park

Home for Ninety-three Years

3

Hyde Park . . . was an articulate, highly organized community, active and effective in civic, educational, political and social affairs.

Julia Abrahamson, *A Neighborhood Finds Itself*

I FELL IN love with a city as some do a sport or the theater or even a writer. How and why did it happen? I don't know entirely, but I think it started in 1911, when I was three years old. My parents, younger sister, and I moved from 4127 South Michigan Avenue to 5488 South Everett Avenue, next to Lake Michigan, and into the Chicago neighborhood of Hyde Park. While I am not always certain of what affected me most, I know that my lake and my neighborhood have continued to have a good effect upon me throughout my life. I have now for ninety-three years been a resident of Hyde Park.

When I was little, I mispronounced my name as "Len," and it has stuck for the rest of my life. I also answer cheerfully to "Leon."

The front room of our apartment in 1911 overlooked a huge lot, and then nothing but Lake Michigan. On clear mornings, the sun rose like a large ball of red fire over the lake. On the lot was nothing but a commercial fisherman's shack. In the winter, he let his fellow fishermen park their boats next to it. Evenings, a city lamplighter would come by to turn on the gas street lights, just the way Larry the Lamplighter did in Robert Louis Stevenson's *Child's Garden of Verses*.

Those years were still the age of the horse. The internal combustion engine had not yet taken over our city. Because there were not many automobiles, there was always plenty of parking.

The lively part of living in Hyde Park was in the backyards and the alleys. The alleys were full of horse-drawn wagons. Fifty-fifth Street for a mile from Cornell Avenue to Cottage Grove Avenue was lined with shops on both sides, and each grocery store had its own delivery wagon. We did not know it then, but Fifty-fifth Street was grandfather to today's shopping malls.

The grocery wagons made deliveries every day. Other wagons carried coal to heat the dwellings, blowing cinders into our eyes. Ice wagons were driven by leather-aproned men who carried cakes of ice according to the signs the lady of the house would put in the window. These announced whether she wanted twenty-five, fifty, or a hundred pounds of ice that day. Junkmen called out, "Rags, old iron." Horse-drawn wagons were used by peddlers of all kinds, especially those who sold fruits and vegetables, specialties they had bought at the South Water Market. Scissors grinders used hand carts with ringing bells.

Then there were musicians who came into the backyards to garner a few coins. They sang Irish songs or Italian operatic arias until they had filled their pockets from all whom they could stimulate. Hurdy-gurdies just played tunes, and organ grinders cranked out songs, accompanied by monkeys who doffed their caps when you gave them a coin.

Pedestrian peddlers carried large baskets of fruits or vegetables. All day long their cries filled the air, but especially in the mornings, very much like the opening scenes of the French opera *Louise*.

The atmosphere in which I lived included books, spectator politics, music, and family adulation. All but the music took hold. Music was reserved for my sister Claire, who later was to become a talented professional musician.

The books came from my maternal great-grandfather, Francis Kiss, a bookbinder by trade. After he came to Chicago from Austria-Hungary, he bought and beautifully bound hundreds, if not thousands, of books in English, German, and French. They were the classics of those nations. Most of them my own family eventually owned. From an early age, even before I could understand them, I read their pages avidly.

The spectator politics came from my father, a staunch Democrat with populist leanings. He followed politics closely, read the newspapers, and discussed the issues of the day. A volunteer speaker for Mayor Carter Harrison II's campaigns, he was appointed twice to the board of directors of the Chicago Public Library. On my part, I was proud of seeing his name in print in the monthly bulletins from the library.

The personal adulation came from another source. My arrival in the world followed two complicated pregnancies that were deep disappointments to my parents, and thus I was a little overvalued as a child and subjected to praise beyond my worth. This hyperbole pleased me as a child, and I have not completely lost the taste for it.

Both my parents were born in this country, but all four of my grandparents arrived from Europe. My paternal grandparents were born in northeastern France, in Lorraine. My maternal grandparents were from the Austro-Hungarian Empire; my grandmother, from Slovakia; and my grandfather, from the Banat (now part of Romania).

When my parents wanted to keep something from me, they conversed in French, to which I owe a lifelong interest in France and French culture. Both of my maternal grandparents were German speaking. My mother spoke German well and taught me the language. In my early childhood, we had newly arrived immigrant German governesses at about seven dollars a week, and I also learned my German from them. French always intrigued me, but German allowed me to keep some things from my father.

The schools of Hyde Park remain a special part of my life. When I was five and a half, my mother, who was always after me to work and to advance, enrolled me in the Elmwood School. It was a small private school with classrooms on Fifty-third Street and a large boardinghouse at the northeast corner of Fifty-fifth Street and Cornell Avenue. There I learned to read. It opened the world of the books that surrounded me at home.

Next, I entered the Ray School, a public one, and was advanced by two years almost at once. This gave me a great advantage, as well as a disadvantage, for I was generally the smallest boy in the class and lagged markedly in sports.

At age eight, I was sent to the University of Chicago elementary school, which still profited from the influence of John Dewey, one of its founders. Again, my mother had thought I was not working hard enough and needed stronger stimuli. I got the stimuli all right. The school was tough. While I had no trouble with memorizing in the public schools, the U. of C. schools demanded creativity, originality, and fresh approaches to material.

In our first year, we studied the English defeat of the Spanish Armada. We not only learned history but also built Kenilworth Castle in our sandbox. We wrote and presented a play about Sir Francis Drake and Queen Elizabeth and composed an article for a magazine, which the students printed and sent to students receiving a comparable education in Great Britain. Work was hard.

I would have liked to stay on in the University of Chicago's elementary and high schools, but in the spring of 1919, I contracted a streptococcus infection and nearly died. As a result, I had to drop out for the entire spring quarter. To avoid losing a full year, I transferred to the Ray School. The principal there used a one-sentence test to place me in the eighth grade.

"Leon, how do you figure the area of a circle?" he asked.

"Pi r squared," I answered, and he placed me in eighth grade.

Hyde Park High School, my next school, was a great joy. The classes were not difficult, and the extracurricular activities proved marvelous for me. I made the extemporaneous speaking and debating teams. I would have liked to win a letter in athletics, but my talents were in public speaking.

Both the Ray School and Hyde Park High School were above average. The teachers were not as stimulating as at the University of Chicago, but they motivated me nevertheless. And in the public schools there were blacks. The University of Chicago school excluded blacks. The public ones I attended did not. As a result, early in my life, I had peer contact with African Americans. At the Ray School, Alonzo Meade and I became friends and stayed so for as long as he lived. At Hyde Park High School there were many more blacks. Although they were prevented from moving to Hyde Park, there were several Hyde Park blocks where their grandparents had settled earlier and they could not be dislodged. I am sorry that I was not then aware of the rigid racial exclusion, but I tried to make up for it later, and so did others in the community of Hyde Park.

In the beginning of 1919 at age ten, almost eleven, I had a very sad experience which shaped my life. My father died. His death occurred at home after a long, long painful bout with cancer. He had been born in Constantine, Michigan. His father, my grandfather, was a stone mason and well digger who eked out a living while raising seven children. His wife died in childbirth.

At age fifteen, my father had to leave home. Sent to Elma, Iowa, to a relative who operated a men's clothing store, he remained in the men's clothing business until near the end of his life. Part of his work consisted of traveling through Iowa and Nebraska. He sometimes did so for ten or eleven weeks at a time, toting trunks loaded with samples. He made close friends with his customers, and for years, both before and after his death, some of them would come to visit us from Iowa and Nebraska. In his last years, he was depressed as a result of his illness but also because he had not made as much money as his peers. One of these was Julius Rosenwald, who headed Sears, Roebuck and Company. They had worked together in Omaha, Nebraska, in a retail clothing store.

My father's death was a great loss to me. In the autumn following it, I entered the confirmation class at Chicago Sinai Congregation, a Reform Jewish congregation. I had attended Sunday school there for several years and was impressed by the rabbi, Emil G. Hirsch, whom I recognized as a great man. He was our Saturday morning teacher for the confirmation class. Although he did not come every week, I looked forward to his being there and felt that it was a privilege to have him as a teacher. He helped make up for the absence of a male figure in my life.

On the first Saturday, Rabbi Hirsch dictated a sentence to us. He asked us to write it down in our notebooks: "Man is made in the image of God." This seemed to me a very ennobling statement and added a great dignity to my conception of myself. Years later I thought that he was also telling us, "God is made in the image of man." But that came much later.

On a subsequent Saturday, he dictated a sentence to us that all people are entitled to equal opportunity regardless of birth or color. The whole year of study with him proved crucial. He instilled the idea that the individual is responsible for his or her own conduct and cannot escape responsibility by reliance on vicarious atonement. He really represented the ideas of the prophets of Israel. When the sanctuary for Sinai Congregation had been built in 1912, he instructed that the facade be inscribed with the words "Mine house shall be a house of prayer for all nations."

AGAIN, when I was fourteen, my mother wonderfully intervened in my life. Just as she had determined that at age five and a half I must learn to read and at age eight that I needed to go to a tougher school, when I was fourteen she decided that I was not working hard enough.

My mother, also one of seven children, was an accomplished musician. Before marriage she had earned her living as a piano teacher, going from one pupil's house to another. She had met my father when she was twelve years old, fell in love with him, but did not see him again until 1903, when she was twenty-seven and he was forty-one. But the die was cast for them. They became engaged on October 3, married on December 24, and lived together until he died at age fifty-six.

She was correct about my not working hard enough, but what a brave thing she proposed and executed in 1922. She announced that we were going to Europe for two years so I could be schooled in a foreign language and have the challenge this would entail. We sailed across the Atlantic, landing in Naples.

In the first week of our European stay, I had an extraordinary aesthetic experience. A trip to see the Greek temple at Paestum, Italy, was a dramatic revelation to me. This magnificent, beautiful building with its marvelous weathered columns stood almost alone in a field covered with red poppies. All was rendered brilliant by a dazzling sun. I had never imagined such a thing. My whole horizon was lifted.

All the rest of our Italian tour offered parallel experiences. I saw things of such unutterable beauty that an interest in art and architecture was kindled in me which has never left. If that were all that happened in Europe, it would have been enough.

Vienna, where we had some acquaintances or friends, was, nevertheless, depressing. It was in the throes of postwar inflation and consequent poverty. We found it distressing just to be there and walk in the streets. My mother decided to return to Rome.

By great good fortune, she was able to enroll me in the Lycée Chateaubriand, a French-government high school established in Rome primarily for French boys and for non-Italians. The school's boarding facility was operated by French monks, and, from the first day, I was immersed in French. Despite two years of French at Hyde Park High School, I could not even understand the monk when he told me the identification number to sew in my clothing.

The boys from the school asked me where I had come from and I said, "America." One of them shocked me a little when he asked,

"Which America?" He was Brazilian and would become a fast friend. Years later he would serve as the top curator of paintings for the Vatican.

It was a wonderful year, and the principal of the school thought I had made enough progress in my French that he would write a letter supporting my admission to the class of *première* at the Lycée Henri IV in Paris. *Première* was the approximate equivalent of senior high school.

Both years in Rome and in Paris were challenging and taxing. In Paris I was again a boarder and immersed in French. Mornings, we were awakened by a drum roll at six o'clock and stayed at school until nine o'clock at night, with two hours for recreation and one and a half hours for meals. We had five hours of class and passed the rest of the time in our study hall. I learned habits of work that have never left me. We ate our meals in the basement of the Romanesque monastery that had preceded the lycée, occasionally had horsemeat, and every evening had a glass of wine. I never drank the wine until my very last day, when I tried it with water. I would always give my glass to one of the other boys. I remember one of them saying to me across the table, "The United States will never be important. It is too far away."

In both Rome and Paris, I endured anti-American feeling and some invective, but generally the comradeship was genuine and pleasant. The classical education was superb. At the end of the year, I took the French baccalaureate examination, first part, and passed. As a precaution, I also took College Board examinations in Paris to make sure I would be admitted to an American university.

AT THE end of two and a half years in Europe, the Despres family sailed back to Chicago. Next came five years at the University of Chicago for my bachelor of arts and a law degree. Many of the courses I took proved both exciting and memorable. The far more attractive features of the university were the stimulating mixture of community, lectures, clubs, and societies; the French and Italian plays I acted in; and the open stacks of the library and the serendipity that came from wandering in them. I greatly enjoyed my fellow students, the discussions we had, and the flow of ideas. In law school also, the essence of the university continued to enrich my very being.

A young female friend, Marian Alschuler, transferred from Vassar to Chicago, principally so we could be together. Fortunately she had one of her philosophy courses in the law school, so for a time we could see each other every day. Our relationship soon deepened, and three years later, we were married.

In 1929, I graduated from law school and was fortunate to land a job in the Sonnenschein law firm, then the second largest in Chicago. It was well run, with high professional standards. My five years there provided excellent training, but I chafed under the organizational restraints. In fact, until just a few years ago, I had recurring nightmares that I was still working there. People used to ask me, "How do you like working in a factory?" The firm consisted of thirty-two lawyers. Today Sonnenschein has around three hundred lawyers and is no longer the second largest in Chicago. I was fortunate to have a salaried job during the depths of the Depression.

The firm did not engage in any pro bono work. I do not know of any other one that did either. I began to have contact with the Chicago Civil Liberties Committee, then an affiliate of the American Civil Liberties Union. Although I could not handle any cases, I could look up law, interview witnesses, and help in other ways. In 1931, an incident occurred that ignited my interest in and ardor for civil liberties. The CCLC asked two other lawyers and me to act as witnesses one Saturday afternoon when the Communist Party planned to picket the Tribune Tower, then the site of the Japanese consulate, in protest against the Japanese occupation of Manchuria. I was not much interested in Manchuria, but rather in watching the demonstration. It began as peacefully as one could imagine, but soon the police waded in and began beating and pursuing the demonstrators. Not satisfied with breaking up the demonstration and beating the participants, they also ran after and continued hitting them, especially demonstrators who stumbled and could not move. This incident horrified me and set on fire a zeal for the defense of free expression.

THE YEAR 1931 marked my marriage to Marian Alschuler. Our relationship has been the crowning experience of my life. Now in its seventy-third year, we are immensely grateful for the fate that has kept us together in such remarkable love and companionship. We had two children, Linda in 1936 and Robert in 1940, a great joy.

In 1932, I felt the urge to engage in politics and made up my mind that I should make a concession to "reality" and become active in the Democratic Party. I obtained a letter of introduction and attended a meeting of the Fifth Ward Democratic Party. Several hundred people were gathered on the top floor of the Piccadilly Hotel in Hyde Park at the regular ward meeting of political workers. I found the group intensely interested not in the great issues of the day but in patronage.

"There are a lot of plums ready for us," said the ward committeeman Horace Lindheimer, "and if you work hard, you will get some of them."

What a ghastly aim of government, the plums of patronage! This was my last expedition to "reality."

After the election, I joined the Socialist Party.

Hyde Park gave me a chance to engage in radical politics. The Socialist Party had a branch in Hyde Park and in a few other parts of Chicago. My four years in the SP were invaluable. I gained lifelong friendships. I understood the mechanism of politics. I developed my speaking skills. I participated in several aldermanic campaigns. In 1936, I took part in the general election. When I left the party in 1937, already somewhat tired of it, I was a much more mature and better-informed person.

Labor organizations began knocking at my door. Both Marian and I took part in picketing. The Italian Bread Drivers League asked me to represent them, but being with a large business law firm, I could not do so and had to turn the work over to a young lawyer named Joseph Jacobs. It formed the nucleus of what became for him a brilliantly successful labor practice.

In 1934, Sonnenschein and I finally separated. I had enough private business to keep me alive, and I gained the freedom to handle the labor and civil rights cases that really enthralled me. They were often pro bono cases, with some fees coming from the labor work. The year 1934 and the years that followed were the beginning of a great labor awakening in the United States, and I took part in some of it. Particularly in 1937, thanks to the warm recommendation by Paul Douglas, then a professor of economics at the University of Chicago and later a U.S. senator, I became the lawyer for Willard Saxby Townsend and the International Brotherhood of Red Caps. This was a wonderfully rewarding experience for me because it gave me a close friendship with Bill Townsend and enabled me to work with him to build a labor organization out of nothing. Redcaps, who handled baggage in railroad stations, were regarded as "privileged trespassers" and received no wages and no recognition from the railroads. My experience lasted for more than twenty years, until the decline of railroad passenger travel meant the end of the organization as an independent body.

I began taking part in antidiscrimination activities. In 1937 I joined with others in a membership campaign to end the color bar in the university's Quadrangle Club. In 1943, I took part in picketing and in lawsuits to open the racial doors of the White City Roller Skating Rink. I mention only a few of the cases that were especially interesting.

In the community in 1948, after the Supreme Court outlawed racial restrictive covenants, we formed the Hyde Park–Kenwood Community Conference. Although in 1931 and until about 1935, I had been working on civil liberties cases with the Chicago Civil Liberties Committee, I was repelled by the Stalinist Communist line of its permanent secretaries: first Tom McKenna and then Ira Latimer. I withdrew from CCLC in favor of working with labor groups and antidiscrimination activities. Finally, the national ACLU became embarrassed by the Stalinist partisanship of the Chicago bureaucracy and initiated the Illinois Division of ACLU with stalwarts who had finally become disillusioned. I had become disillusioned much earlier because my experience in the Socialist Party had inoculated me against the Stalinist virus. I had had experience with "united fronts" and other divisive and deceptive Stalinist practices. When the Chicago group asked me to be vice chairman, I readily accepted and quickly became counsel, pro bono, a position I held and worked on actively for seven years until I ran for alderman in 1955.

The year 1948 was the one in which two other lawyers and I tried the case of James Hickman, a dramatic murder case involving racial housing segregation in Chicago.

Marian was also active in the community in an effective way, different from mine but along similar lines when the opportunity offered. In 1943 Marian Despres, along with Fruma Gottschalk, mounted a campaign to open the University of Chicago Laboratory Schools to individuals of African American descent. The principal refused, saying, "They would not be happy here."

When Robert M. Hutchins, the president of the university, was approached, he was indifferent. Marian and Fruma mobilized parents to sign petitions, searched out black parents who agreed to enroll their children in the school, and kept the matter alive until finally they succeeded.

I ONCE tried to escape from Hyde Park. It wasn't that I disliked the neighborhood. I was pleased with almost everything about it. I liked its openness to radical ideas, new currents of thought, and thoughtful conceptions of equality. I thought I found one problem with Hyde Park. I came to the conclusion that the public schools were not as good as those in the north suburbs. I decided that we ought to try Winnetka to see if we did not owe it to our children to move there or to some similar suburb. We were fortunate to rent a house in Winnetka on the lakeshore and spend the summer there. It took only a few days to change my mind. We attended the Fourth of July celebration on the village green, and there I saw large numbers of suburbanites. I recognized a few lawyers whom I disliked. I noticed that the whole assemblage was totally white and upper-middle class. It was no place for us. My escape from Hyde Park came to an abrupt end. Although we found neighbors in Winnetka who were congenial, we realized that the suburbs were not for us, and our escape adventure terminated decisively.

I felt forever indebted to Paul Cornell, who had founded Hyde Park in 1856 and laid it out as an independent village. He took full advantage of its geographical asset as a self-contained lakefront community, adorned it with magnificent parks, and connected it to the central city by extraordinary transportation facilities. It was annexed by Chicago in 1889. I am still in love with Hyde Park and all Paul Cornell did to make it possible.

Urban Nature at My Doorstep

4

*It may have a beauty and an interest of its own, in which
citizens of Chicago for generations to come shall take pride,
and all the more so that it has been the result of their fathers'
pride upon a sandbar.*

Frederick Law Olmsted and Calvert Vaux, from an 1871 letter
proposing what would become Jackson Park

IF MY SOUL is closely united with the community of Hyde Park, it is
indissolubly attached to its jewel on the lake, Jackson Park. I am last-
ingly grateful to Paul Cornell, who more than a century and a half
ago lobbied for the bond issue that bought the land, and to Frederick
Law Olmsted for landscaping it.

The earliest photograph taken of me was in Jackson Park, at the
age of six months, lying on the grass, with my beloved maternal
grandmother watching over me. Jackson Park was where my father
used to take me on Sunday-morning walks. One sunny spring day
when I was in kindergarten, the carriage drove all the children to
Jackson Park for a delicious picnic of bread-and-butter sandwiches.
In that same spring, my upstairs neighbor invited me to a church
picnic. With happy, laughing young parents I sat in a large circle
on the grass near what was then the Field Museum and is now the
Museum of Science and Industry. I wished then that my family went
to church, too.

Automobiles were still a novelty in my childhood, and one favorite recreation was to be taken for a motor spin in Jackson Park along
the lake. The South Park commissioners posted a speed limit of
twenty miles per hour.

I loved walking out on the piers with my father as far as we could go into the lake. The piers were left over from the years when steamboats ran between Jackson Park and downtown. Near the piers was a beautiful replica of a River Rhine castle, the German Building, which remained from the 1893 World's Fair. I appreciated its beauty, but even more the ice cream sodas I would be treated to inside.

THE GERMAN BUILDING was nothing next to the three Japanese buildings on the Wooded Island, also left over from the World's Fair. I could run around their porches, and I think I did so for hours. They were exquisite and had attracted the artistic eye of Frank Lloyd Wright. Just beyond the Wooded Island was the one-room Cahokia County Court House, which was later returned to Cahokia, Illinois. The Japanese buildings were burned by a "patriotic" vandal soon after Pearl Harbor.

In the spring, the roses in the garden on the Wooded Island bloomed and cast their perfume into the air. Each year I loved them. Today's roses are comparatively scentless.

The lagoons were a source of pleasure, summer and winter. Rowboats were for rent, and I learned to steer and to row, first with older people, and then on my own. The boats were particularly valuable when I was courting the young woman who became my wife. I remember a wonderful night ride we took next to the museum. Very romantic. In the winter the lagoons froze over and, from the warming house, I could step out and skate all the way around the Wooded Island and back.

THE FORMER Palace of Fine Arts left over from the World's Fair was then the Field Museum, a treasure house. From early childhood I went there often, especially on Sundays in the winter, sometimes alone and other times with a friend. We explored everything, all the stuffed animals, the Indian exhibits, the Chinese exhibits, and particularly the Hall of Gems and Jewels, where we thought the exhibits were worth millions and millions of dollars.

In the summer of my tenth year, I played golf on the nine-hole course, now gone. In that year, I also accompanied my father on the eighteen-hole course.

At the south end of Hyde Park is a place called La Rabida. It served then as a hospital for tubercular children, but my elders explained that it had been a World's Fair replica of the convent where Christopher Columbus and his son took refuge. I could almost see them, but I could certainly view Columbus's three caravel replicas in the harbor, the Niña, the Pinta, and the Santa Maria. In 1915, when I was seven, they towed the boats away to San Francisco for the exposition. I missed them. Two of the boats never returned, but years later we welcomed back the Santa Maria, the sole survivor of the round trip.

The park was full of nature's bounty, but not much that grew was edible, except the mulberries in the spring. My elders took me bird watching. Although I found it boring and could not even see the birds they were talking about, my nonchalance was eventually overcome years later, when Douglas Anderson began leading famous bird walks every Wednesday and Saturday morning from March to November.

My FIELD MUSEUM was replanted at the south end of Grant Park in a new building, but the old one got an even more exciting tenant: the Museum of Science and Industry, which became a treasure for my children. They could not go there often enough, especially to the coal mine with its simulated gas explosion. The Museum of Science and Industry soon pulled more visitors than any other Chicago attraction. It needed a parking area, so it ate up the green space north of the building and destroyed the grassy "soup bowl" depression I used to roll down. Lately, the green space has been sanitized and restored over a new underground parking garage.

I Am Told What to Expect in the City Council

5

Which side are you on?
From a 1930s labor song

My FIRST regular session of the city council after my 1955 election was bewildering, even more than I had expected. Clerks kept going back and forth depositing papers on aldermen's desks for signature. The mayor sat on an elevated podium, and the fifty aldermen were in front of him at their desks in three semicircular rows.

How should I vote? How could I avoid showing my ignorance? How could I escape supporting something which would embarrass me later?

The city clerk, who sat below the mayor, called the roll. The aldermen around me seemed to understand whether to vote aye or nay. Some were veterans who knew the score and some were new aldermen who emulated the bellwether, Alderman John D'Arco. Because he was the First Ward alderman, he voted first, and others followed his lead. He always seemed to know how to vote, or at least he followed orders.

Lobbyists from the telephone company, the Chicago Transit Authority, Commonwealth Edison, and others introduced themselves to me graciously.

I had hardly entered the chambers when someone asked if I wanted to enroll in the City of Chicago Pension Fund. I did not expect to serve the twenty years required for vesting a pension, but I thought I owed it to my constituents to enter the plan and evaluate it at firsthand.

At the end of twenty years, I did get my pension. Based on my ultimate salary of eight thousand dollars, it was three hundred dollars a month. Today an alderman's salary is over ninety thousand dollars, with earned pension rights more than ten times mine.

Entering the city council, I believed that to be effective I would have to deal with the deepest problems of Chicago, and I would also have to deliver to constituents, rich and poor, all the services they expected from an alderman.

Chicago was then, as it usually is, burdened with problems and uncertainty. It was governed by a political machine that depended for office on its political patronage. The Democratic organization had thousands of jobs in various countywide offices, which it could fashion into a strong political army. If patronage workers failed to deliver votes, they lost their job or title. In the election campaign, I had just come up against the ardor of that patronage army, which had fought to return me full-time to my law office. The political machine in Chicago tolerated considerable corruption and pursued its enemies relentlessly.

Chicago operated without any comprehensive city plan. I do not mean an exact one for each block, but broad guidelines which looked ahead ten, twenty, and even fifty years. If it had a plan, each major improvement could be judged not only for itself but also by how it fitted the developing city.

This absence of public planning seemed to me to be a dreadful omission, and I had vowed to make working toward a plan one of the most important steps in my legislative agenda. As I sat on the city council that morning, no one else there seemed to be interested in such a concept. The columnist Mike Royko would coin the slogan *Ubi est mea?* (Where is mine?) as the only spur that guided most Machine members' actions.

As the second plank in my program, I placed a goal of eliminating racial segregation and discrimination and protecting civil rights and liberties.

From a Machine alderman sitting behind me, I received a unique welcome to the arena in which I found myself. The Twenty-sixth Ward alderman Mathew Bieszczat (a deeply committed Machine politician) said to me, "I want you to know that if you behave the way Alderman Merriam did, we'll do the same thing to you we did to him." This was said in an angry, hostile manner. What they "did to him" was essentially drive him out, undermine him at every possible point, and finally defeat him for office. I had no doubt of Bieszczat's sincere intention to do the same to me. In a way, his welcome was a reassurance that I had little to lose by adhering steadfastly to my vision for Chicago.

My first day was one of learning what to do, if not how to do it. I realized I would not be obliged to follow the vote of First Ward alderman D'Arco.

Ending the Sale of Driveway Permits

My First Victory

6

Strike while the iron is hot.

Old proverb

At a St. Patrick's Day joint meeting of aldermen and state legislators one year, Mayor Daley responded to an introduction by reciting an Irish wish. It ended with the words "may the wind always be at your back." In my years in the city council, the wind was rarely at my back, but one time it was, and the experience was glorious.

Driveway permits were one of the sordid scourges of the city council. They were an open abuse that went on year after year. There were far graver scandals, like utility franchises, but no more persistent ones. Driveway permits helped give the city council a reputation for corruption.

What is a driveway permit? If you open an automobile service station or a hotel, or if you have a garage at the back of your home, and you want to cut a driveway through the curb and sidewalk so that people can drive into the service station or the hotel or your garage, you have to get a permit from the city to make the cut. Without the permit, your service station or hotel or garage would be inaccessible by car.

For decades driveway permits were the sole responsibility of each alderman, and, as Alderman Thomas Keane said to me privately, "About half the aldermen sell driveway permits." That was an understatement. They had no right to sell driveway permits, but they did so, and the prices went from a few hundred dollars for a backyard garage to thousands of dollars for a hotel. If you wanted to open a multimillion-dollar retail store and needed driveway permits for access, your alderman could hold you up, and frequently did.

When I ran for the city council, I vowed that I would try to get rid of this incubus. I had solid support from the public, but not from the aldermen. Before Mayor Daley took office, his predecessor, the businesslike Martin J. Kennelly, commissioned a series of excellent studies of city government by very competent management firms. He also appointed a group called the Home Rule Commission, made up of businessmen, academicians, and a few representatives of government. Alderman Thomas Keane himself, then chairman of the City Council Committee on Traffic and Public Safety, was a member. The commission issued an excellent report in book form with splendid recommendations for the improvement of Chicago's government, which included abolishing aldermanic driveway permits. The only way to stop aldermen from accepting such bribes was to take away from them the power to issue driveway permits.

After I entered the city council, I asked some of the Republican aldermen to join in an ordinance to remedy this scourge, but I could not get them to do so. This was not because the competent Republican aldermen I approached were necessarily taking money. Rather, the aldermen who had long been in the city council and had long hoped to eliminate the scourge were basically tired of continuing the attack. They were also reluctant to incur the wrath of their colleagues who wanted the boodle. At that time, an alderman's salary was five thousand dollars a year, and the driveway permit income was a nice addition for the half of the city council described by Alderman Keane as being on the take.

I set to work, talked to the head of the Home Rule Commission staff, and with help from the commission's attorney wrote a good draft for a driveway permit ordinance, taking the power away from the aldermen and giving it to the executive branch.

When Alderman Keane found out, he encouraged me to go ahead. In itself that was a fresh wind at my back. The problem then was to get the item on the city council agenda. If the ordinance were publicized in advance, it would be throttled. I felt I had to devise a way to get it introduced without its being noticed.

The wind was favorable, but I had to tack. At each council meeting, when an alderman proposed legislation, a slip of paper with a title would be placed on the proposed ordinance, and the clerk who stood in front of the mayor would intone what was going through his hands. I can almost hear him saying, "Order for a canopy, amendment to the zoning ordinance, a couple of driveway permits, an ordinance to rename a street, another driveway permit," and so on. I mixed my driveway reorganization ordinance in with the other miscellaneous papers I was presenting and labeled it simply "Driveway Permits." The slip was truthful, but when the clerk called out "Driveway permits," no one realized that it was much more than just a routine order for specific permits. It was actually an earthshaking attack on the aldermanic payoffs.

At the end of the council meeting, when the newspaper reporters pored over what had been introduced, they became very excited. *Daily News* reporter Jay McMullen, who later married Jane Byrne, rushed over to me and said, "Len, did you really introduce an ordinance to take away driveway permits from the city council?"

A moment later Alderman Harry Sain, whom the press had referred to as "Hot Stove Sain," the chairman of the committee on driveway permits, asked the same question. He said, "Alderman, if I had known that that was the ordinance you were introducing, I would have called it up immediately and we would have voted on it at once." What a nice offer! He would have called it up for an immediate vote so that he could kill it. There was nothing they could do. The ordinance was now on the city council agenda.

It soon became apparent that the mayor liked the ordinance, which no regular alderman had wanted to introduce. He did so because he was interested in strengthening the executive branch. He was a re-former, but always in the direction of increasing his power as mayor. I never knew him to support any reform that decreased the mayor's power. He was always enthusiastic about improving city government if it gave him more power. He understood and loved power. And he did all he could to increase his own.

On the morning of the city council vote on my ordinance, I asked Alderman Keane whether it would pass. "You make sure the Republican aldermen vote for it," he said, "and I'll take care of the rest."

I had no power over the Republican aldermen, but I knew that the good-government aldermen like John Hoellen, Einar Johnson, and Allen Freeman would vote for it. They were all committed to it, but there were also "Republican" aldermen who were only Republicans to get votes and in reality were Machine aldermen in cozy relationships, and I wasn't sure of them. In addition, there were many aldermen who did not want to give up the income from driveway permits. The ordinance carried, but it did so by the close vote of twenty-eight to twenty, with two absences. This represented a formidable in-house opposition to the mayor, and it was the last time such resistance ever occurred under Mayor Richard J. Daley. It was the final audible gasp of Gray Wolves, as the famous muckraker journalist Lincoln Steffens had labeled the corrupt members of the Chicago City Council in 1912.

In this case, I had had the wind at my back and it had brought me safely to my destination.

Richard J. Daley

An Overrated Powerhouse

7

> *Years later, [Alderman] Keane would distill the difference*
> *between himself and [Mayor] Daley to a simple choice:*
> *Daley had spent his career pursuing power, Keane said,*
> *while he had always pursued money.*

Adam Cohen and Elizabeth Taylor, *American Pharaoh*

For twenty years Richard J. Daley and I faced each other in the Chicago City Council. He presided over the fifty-alderman body, and I sat directly under his dais. I saw him many other times also but rarely on a one-to-one basis.

Mayor Daley was interested, even obsessed, with getting and holding political power. By a long, patient, consistent effort he achieved his goal, probably beyond his original dreams. As a youth, he entered the business of politics. Many other young men living in his neighborhood, Bridgeport, went into real estate, sheet metal work, lumber, or the stockyards, but Richard J. Daley went into the business of politics for the rest of his life.

He became a protégé of Joseph McDonough, the Eleventh Ward Democratic committeeman, and filled a variety of political jobs and offices from early adulthood on. He was a conscientious and hard worker. James Cusack, Fifth Ward alderman from 1935 to 1939, told me that in those years when Richard J. Daley was clerk to the city council, he was accommodating, intelligent, careful, and ready whenever necessary to stay beyond regular hours.

He worked his way up through the political hierarchy and finally in 1953 got himself elected chairman of the Democratic Organization of Cook County by the fifty ward committeemen from Chicago and the thirty township committeemen from the rest of Cook County. The chairmanship was his important, lifetime position. If we had been technical about his title in terms of power, we would have referred to him not as "Mayor Daley" but as "Chairman Daley." As chairman he essentially controlled the Democratic Party of Cook County, selected candidates, placated and scolded ward and township committeemen, and commanded a patronage army that rose to about forty-five thousand.

Daley sought and obtained not power over the city but power over a political organization. That is what interested him. He wanted to control the party, all the local offices, and as many state and federal ones as possible. He did not rule the city; he ruled the governments in the city. The authors of *American Pharaoh* concluded that he was perhaps the most powerful local official in any big city in the United States. But he was not an emperor.

When I first met Daley in 1954, he had already become chairman of the Democratic Party of Cook County. I was chairman of the Adoption Law Committee of the Chicago Bar Association and went to see him in his capacity as county clerk about a change of procedures in the county court. We wanted the court to follow a protective procedure for docketing adoption cases.

County Clerk Daley impressed me immediately as a strong person but not a particularly articulate one. He quickly assented to our suggestion but said that he did not want to have the county court reform its procedure alone. He asked us to obtain the same commitment from the circuit court and the superior court. I respected his willingness to adopt an improvement and his intelligence in making the commitment conditional for his own protection.

Daley remodeled his private office as county clerk to give it luxury and impressiveness suitable for a party chairman. For the rest of his career, he pursued this practice of having an impressive office. Naturally, when we met in 1954 neither of us thought that we would be spending twenty years looking at each other across the well of the Chicago City Council Chamber.

Richard J. Daley had some amazing characteristics. He was clearly devoted to his family. He took care of them in public employment. The *Chicago Tribune* conducted a retrospective survey in 1989 showing that over a forty-four-year span that included the twenty-one years of Richard J. Daley's mayoralty as well as nine years of his son's (Richard M. Daley), sixty-eight of their relatives had served on the public payroll. *Tribune* reporters used the Freedom of Information Act as well as "census and court records, death notices, and newspaper clips" to compile the data.

Daley made it a practice to take dinner with his family every night. This was a wise practice for him, them, and his digestion. The mayor frequently appeared at large public dinners, after he had eaten at home.

Daley was devoted to the Roman Catholic Church. He had been an altar boy and was a serious practicing Catholic. I was once astounded to see him greet the cardinal. He went quickly to his knees, took the cardinal's hand, kissed his ring, and then stood up and began talking to him. His religion was of paramount importance to him, but he did not hesitate to disagree politically with the church, if necessary. When the archdiocese under Cardinal Albert Meyer sharply criticized the city's Hyde Park–Kenwood urban renewal plan for not providing enough affordable housing, Daley ignored the attack and continued on his course without modification.

The mayor depended for his strength on the patronage system. At the height of his power he controlled forty-five thousand jobs. These were all listed on card catalogs in the party office, with annotations showing the committeeman to whom the job was charged. By granting or withholding patronage, Daley kept the committeemen under his thumb. When he deposed Committeeman William Dawson from control of any ward except the Second, he did so in a very simple way. He froze the Fourth Ward patronage, thus giving the appearance that he was impartial in a clash between Dawson and Fourth Ward committeeman Holman. But by freezing the patronage, he destroyed Dawson's power to hire and fire, which Dawson had enjoyed for years. The conflict was quickly resolved in favor of Holman, who then became a full-fledged Fourth Ward committeeman, handling his ward's patronage without subservience to the Second Ward committeeman.

Daley was a strong and autocratic party chairman, but he had genuine warmth and loyalty for his own in-group within the party. He watched over his distribution of largesse. My friend Harry Iseberg handled liquor license revocation cases for years and carefully protected the mayor from any scandals. When Iseberg saw Daley once, the mayor said to him without prompting, "Harry, I know what you want and I'm going to take care of you." Soon thereafter Harry became a judge.

If committeemen disagreed with each other and the fight was a hard one, Daley stepped in and supported the side that would bring him more strength. He did so in the patronage quarrel between Holman and Dawson. He acted also in a tiff between Alderman Thomas Keane and County Board president Seymour Simon. Simon had conscientiously refused to go along with a project dear to Keane, who was Daley's floor leader and a big vote getter in his ward. The two committeemen were at loggerheads, and the mayor gave in to Keane and took Simon off the ticket. Nearly always, Daley was able to mediate or conciliate differences by the use of his power, specifically by using the appointments and jobs at his disposal.

BEING chairman of the Cook County organization was the realization of his ambition, but it was never enough. When selected as chairman, he had obtained party power. The mayor's office was a position that carried with it so much governmental power and so many jobs that he could not feel secure simply as party chairman. He felt, indeed he knew, he also had to hold the job of mayor. Consequently, as 1955 approached, Daley arranged for the party to supplant the sitting mayor, Kennelly, even though he had twice been elected with the full support of the Democratic organization.

When Richard J. Daley became mayor while remaining party chairman, he had really achieved the summit of his ambition. He had an unusual reverence for the chief municipal office. Once in the course of a discussion on the floor of the city council, I alluded to a disreputable practice of former mayor Edward Kelly (1933–47). From the chair, Daley interrupted me to say, "We do not criticize former mayors."

At the beginning of his mayoralty tenure, Daley was tentative and overwhelmed by the power of the office. Nothing stopped him from immediately enlarging the number of temporary employees who could be appointed on a patronage basis. Still, he was slow to take the kind of totalitarian control of the city council and the government that he would achieve a year later. Thus, his first year as mayor was so congenial that it was possible to operate in the city council with some freedom, originate legislation, and raise objections that received attention. That came to an end after about a year, when Daley became extremely authoritarian.

His position as mayor and party chairman gave him tight control of governmental offices and allowed him to negotiate on an almost equal basis with the rulers of finance and commerce. It certainly put him in a strong position to raise funds and handle them discreetly.

As mayor, he showed considerable ability in dealing with public finance. Daley had been finance director for the State of Illinois under Governor Adlai Stevenson. He had both the talent and the skill to handle public finances. His budgets were carefully framed. He understood how to get money for the operation of city government, where to find new sources, and how to administer funds.

The mayor loved public works, seeing to it that there were lots of them, with contracts, jobs, and campaign contributions. He made certain that what was produced was of good quality even though expensive. In his book *Don't Make No Waves, Don't Back No Losers*, Milton Rakove quotes Studs Terkel as saying of Daley: "He's marvelous when it comes to building things like highways, parking lots, and industrial complexes. But when it comes to healing the aches and hurts of human beings, he comes up short."

Daley had a talent for choosing able people to run the government, or at least for planting his own eyes and ears in positions to check on department heads' performances. Among outstanding department heads, he named Carl Chatters, a national expert in public finance, as controller and Earl Bush as his public relations man.

Bush was extraordinarily capable in guiding Daley, protecting him, handling his publicity, creating an image, advising him, and building a mythic legend around the man. Daley owed much of his success as mayor to the skill with which Bush supported the mayor's position, until the public relations man himself got into trouble with the federal government. He had used his office to obtain a lucrative airport contract.

In the technical dispensation of city services Daley regarded himself as mayor of all the people. He did not, as Mayor Kelly had done, withhold garbage collection in reprisal for unpleasant activities. He neglected whole areas of the city, but he did not specifically deny any basic services.

His public statements did not have the faithfulness of his private commitments. When he ran for county clerk in 1954, he promised that he would serve out his full four-year term. He probably had no intention of doing so and ran for mayor in 1955. When he campaigned for mayor, he promised he would step down as party chairman. He had no intention of doing so, was elected mayor, and remained party chairman for the rest of his life.

He had a terrible temper, which he kept under control most of the time. His outstanding loss of it in the Chicago City Council occurred when Alderman Dick Simpson referred to Daley's favoritism in giving city business to his son's insurance agency. Daley launched a tirade that continued nonstop for more than fifteen minutes. He urged everyone who disagreed with his favoritism toward his son to "kiss his mistletoe."

Another outstanding public loss of temper occurred at the 1968 Democratic National Convention, when he was caught on television in a rage after Senator Abraham Ribicoff referred to the "Gestapo tactics of the Chicago police." Lip readers said Daley had uttered a crude obscenity.

Sometimes he would lose his temper at press conferences. It was on one such occasion that public relations director Bush told reporters, "Don't report what he says, report what he means."

Daley had a talent for assembling winning tickets. He lost some elections but won some outstanding ones. He had no special love for Adlai Stevenson III. One Sunday Stevenson invited people publicly to his Libertyville farm to launch a new political group. To my astonishment, Daley arrived at the gathering to speak. When Stevenson rose to introduce Daley, I grasped what had happened. Adlai said that his father "would have rejoiced at the unity that had just been achieved in the party." What had occurred was that Daley had learned in the afternoon that Senator Everett M. Dirksen had died and that the coming election for U.S. Senate would not therefore be endangered by Dirksen's strong Republican vote-getting presence. Daley, as a result, offered the senatorial nomination to Stevenson, who would be a tremendous vote getter at the head of a ticket and would sweep in the Democratic candidates under him.

On another occasion, when the Illinois Supreme Court adjudicated a legal challenge to legislative districting, directing that the election of state representatives be at large, Daley built a strong ticket by inviting Abner Mikva to run again. By agreeing Mikva obtained commitment of a valuable chairmanship for himself. Again, the presence of an attractive candidate swept in the party's favorites.

Daley had respect for dissidents in the party who showed strength. In one party primary election Edward Vrdolyak, an annoying right-wing alderman, ran against the party candidate for the office of county assessor. Daley's choice got 400,000 votes, and Vrdolyak 200,000. I thought that as head of the party Daley would punish Vrdolyak. Quite the contrary—Daley clearly respected someone who could obtain 200,000 votes, and Vrdolyak was never toppled from his position in the party or in office, at least not by Daley.

The mayor tolerated a wide swath of corruption among office-holders. He required only that the corruption not be publicly abusive and that the individual not be caught. If an individual were caught, Daley cut him off.

When Otto Kerner, a favorite of Daley, was finally convicted and Daley was asked to comment, he simply said, "He shouldn't have taken race track stock." That was the end of Kerner. When Tom Keane, Daley's floor leader in the city council, was indicted for systematically voting on measures in which he had a secret financial interest, Daley stood by him. When he was convicted, it was the end of Tom Keane politically, although Daley said, "He will always be my friend."

Daley had a special weak spot. He never accepted African American Chicagoans on an equal basis. He used their committeemen and officeholders to get votes. He allotted them their mathematical share of patronage. He reserved the highest offices for whites. He resisted a genuine opening of the police and fire departments. He arranged the construction of the Dan Ryan Expressway to serve, he hoped, as a barrier to expansion of black residence. He resisted genuine fair-housing legislation as long as he could.

In his youth he had been a member of the Hamburg Athletic Association, which is mentioned as a probable participant in the 1919 Chicago race riots. He never told what he did at the time of the riots.

He never leveled with Chicago about it. His actions during those race riots have never become public, but the way his peers felt about color prejudice influenced his entire life.

In 1975, Daley ran for mayor for the last time. He had had health problems before then. A prudent man would not have run again. He placed his desire to hold on to power above a sensible decision to retire. It was impossible for him to give up power, so on December 20, 1976, in the first year of his last term, he attended the dedication of a new Southeast Side Chicago Park District gym. He then went to a scheduled appointment at his doctor's office. He died there of a heart attack.

Saving the City's Outdoor Museum

8

Chicago builds itself up, knocks itself down again,
scrapes away the rubble, and starts over. . . .
A Chicagoan as he wanders about the city feels like
a man who has lost many teeth.

Saul Bellow, *It All Adds Up*

In 1955, few Chicagoans knew of or appreciated the city's historic architectural landmarks. Only a handful recognized Chicago's urgent need for the kind of preservation program that had retained and protected historic structures in Athens and Rome and Paris before it was too late to save them. Although architects, historians, and art lovers agonized over the continuing losses of Chicago's internationally significant structures, there were no organizational or governmental efforts to prevent their destruction. A 1956 telephone call made me determined to help bring about a change.

One evening in 1956, Hugh Dalziel Duncan called me from Carbondale, where he was a sociology professor at Southern Illinois University, with an impassioned plea. A former Chicago-area resident, he had studied the city's architecture and written extensively about it. He said that most people simply did not know how great Chicago's treasures were, and he then added, "Chicago is a living outdoor museum of architecture and its treasures are in peril of unregulated demolition." He urged me to become aware of this and to take protective action through the city government. Because of indifference and ignorance, he said, irreplaceable landmarks were on the verge of being destroyed.

47

At the end of the conversation, he said he would send me a copy of his article on the subject and would ask Tom Stauffer to meet with me. Stauffer, a City College instructor and a passionate lover of Chicago's great architecture, more than any other person gave an initial impetus to Chicago's architectural preservation movement.

Duncan apparently sensed that I could be sympathetic to his appeal, or might become so. He was correct. Although poorly informed about Chicago's architectural treasures, I greatly admired Frank Lloyd Wright. I had visited both Taliesins, his homes and studios in Wisconsin and Arizona.

My school days in Italy and France helped make me aware of efforts at architectural and historical preservation in those countries. I realized that the great treasures of their past civilizations were legally protected from defacement or demolition. I loved their wonderful cathedrals, palaces, and other structures. My gratitude extended to everyone who had worked to preserve them, as if for my personal enjoyment. How dreadful it would have been if Notre Dame in Paris had been allowed to crumble or if the Coliseum in Rome had been replaced with a high-rise.

In Buffalo, New York, on a trip east in 1945, eleven years before Hugh Duncan's telephone call, my wife, Marian, and I had walked with sadness amid the ruins of Frank Lloyd Wright's beautiful Larkin Building. Marian's father, Alfred S. Alschuler (1876–1940), a distinguished Chicago architect, had left both of us a legacy of lively interest in architecture. Among the buildings which he designed was the London Guarantee on the southwest corner of Michigan Avenue and Wacker Drive.

I was just beginning then to admire another Chicago architect, Louis Sullivan. I asked an architect friend, "What is so wonderful about Sullivan's Carson Pirie Scott Building? How is it different from any other State Street department store?"

He was irritated. "Next time, look at the flowing horizontal lines," he said, and turned away. When I did look, I saw what he had meant and what Hugh Duncan was saying as well. I had become a fertile recipient for their ideas.

Soon afterward, Tom Stauffer called me, along with Graham Aldis, a real estate agent. We met for lunch at the Bismarck (now the Allegro) Hotel. Aldis was a successful businessman with genuine civic and artistic interest. The Walnut Room, where we met, was crowded daily with political leaders, and over the years undoubtedly incubated many momentous legislative decisions. On that day it served as the birthplace of Chicago's landmark preservation ordinance.

At the luncheon meeting they thoroughly won me over to the need for city council action. Architectural preservation seemed an important step in city planning, then my major aldermanic goal. I sensed that there was not yet enough support to make it legally enforceable, so I agreed to draft a measure for a commission that would simply designate buildings of great worth. It could get city council support, I thought, and would be a big step in making clear which buildings in the city were of greatest worth. Since the designation of worth would not be legally enforceable, it would not arouse opposition.

I took another precaution. I asked Alderman William Murphy, chairman of the Housing and Planning Committee, to join in on the measure. He agreed. With his endorsement, I obtained the same support from Alderman Emil Pacini, chairman of the Zoning Committee. Their sponsorship helped passage in the city council. Alderman Murphy was friendly to me and had a genuine understanding of the value of an architectural preservation commission for the designation of worthy buildings, even if it were not compulsory. At this time, Daley had not yet tightened his control of the city council. Later, without his nod, I could not have obtained the support of an administration alderman for such a measure, however benign. In time the mayor forbade any such cooperation and insisted that all measures of any significance originate with or through the administration.

With two first-rate cosponsors, the measure had city council respectability and assurance of getting at least a good hearing. This was scheduled before the Housing and Planning Committee. We mailed notices to every interested person and organization I could think of.

Tom Stauffer must have worked to stimulate the interest of the Chicago chapter of the American Institute of Architects. On the morning of the hearing about twenty-five architects crowded the hearing room to testify favorably to the importance of the measure.

JOHN ROOT, of the Holabird and Root architectural firm, was the main spokesperson. "We have to find a way to premiate the fine buildings in Chicago," he said. That was exactly what needed to be done. I had never come across "premiate," but he used just the right word because it designated the special status they deserve. No one spoke in opposition. If the measure had had enforcement powers, real estate developers and organizations would almost certainly have opposed it. None did.

It passed. I assumed then that the mayor might want suggestions about who should be on the commission to "premiate" the buildings. No such thing. He was the only one who did any selecting or appointing. He named Daniel Catton Rich of the Art Institute as the first chairman. It was a good commission, free to work to the best of its ability because it was not impinging on any landowner's powers. On the contrary, it was lending distinction to buildings. Daley could afford to name suitable and competent members and give them artistic leeway. The new commission went ahead diligently to identify worthwhile buildings. This was a start. It produced a list of thirty-nine buildings to be designated landmarks.

The creation of the commission gave a healthy stimulus to Chicago's underlying concern for architectural preservation. Stauffer and others had formed the private Chicago Heritage Committee, an interested architectural group that encouraged and supported public preservation activities. The action of the new commission in designating buildings of architectural interest began to awaken the people of Chicago.

The city then operated under the 1870 Illinois Constitution, which limited what a city government could do. Unless a power were specifically granted by the Illinois General Assembly, the city did not have it. This made municipal government difficult. For example, Chicago had long been unable even to regulate rooming houses for lack of a specific grant of power. It could not enact an enforceable preservation ordinance. To remedy this gap, the Metropolitan Housing and Planning Council, a civic organization, had Calvin Sawyier, a lawyer, draft a state law to give Chicago the necessary authority. Still, the city administration did not act on it.

As the work of the noncompulsory commission progressed in "premiating" one building after another, I was astonished to see how much public sentiment surfaced for architectural preservation, and soon thereafter how much opposition. The designation of significant buildings was all well and good, but the drive to tear them down continued.

The very first test over architectural preservation was soon under way. It was the effort of Chicago Theological Seminary to tear down Robie House, designed by Frank Lloyd Wright, and build a student dormitory. Situated in Chicago's Fifth Ward at Fifty-eighth Street and Woodlawn Avenue in Hyde Park, Robie House is one of the city's, if not the country's, greatest architectural treasures.

One day the president of CTS, Arthur Cushman McGiffert, asked me to come to his office. "We think CTS owes it to the alderman of the ward to tell you we are planning to demolish Robie House," he said. "We need the land to build our new dormitory."

Horrified at what I had just heard, I objected, argued, and remonstrated. No use. McGiffert expressed CTS's immediate, immutable, irrevocable determination to destroy the building. As I walked out of his office, I noticed a photograph of the Parthenon on the wall and disingenuously asked him what it was. I commented that we were fortunate that it had not been demolished. McGiffert represented the viewpoint of "I accept architectural preservation, but not for my house."

I had to mobilize opposition immediately. To this end I called Tom Stauffer. He began organizing a brilliant defense of Robie House. Soon there came a barrage of articles, publicity releases, letters, statements, and demonstrators. To lovers of art and architecture, the threat to demolish Robie House was a dreadful possibility. Built in 1909, it is an outstanding example of prairie architecture and is regarded as a unique treasure. Stauffer stimulated American and European architectural groups to pour in their protests.

If they did not understand it before, most Chicagoans, including those connected with CTS and the affiliated University of Chicago, finally grasped Robie's worldwide importance in the history of architecture. I made strong aldermanic noises. Soon CTS and the U. of C. began to look like vandals.

Surprisingly there was also some sentiment, although not organized, in favor of demolition. Maynard Krueger, a faculty friend whom I had supported for alderman in 1935 and for Congress in 1948, told me: "There is no feeling around the university faculty that Robie House needs to be preserved." I think he was reflecting the market views of the Chicago School of Economics and their talk around the Quadrangle Club faculty lunch table.

George Fred Keck, a fine modern architect and profound admirer of Wright, said, "There is no point in trying to save Robie House. We have the complete measurements and photographs. That is the essential. What is important now is to build good new architecture." I was shocked, but I believe Fred was just expressing his irrepressible urge to do creative building.

The campaign's highpoint was Stauffer's arranging a dramatic morning visit to Robie House by Frank Lloyd Wright himself. I think it tipped the scale. The university then realized it should not permit itself, let alone CTS, to perpetrate the Robie House murder (you might have called it aggravated domicide) of a great creation.

As a new-found champion of Robie House, the U. of C. arranged a happy solution. William Zeckendorff, who had a big contract for townhouses, apartment buildings, and a shopping center in the new Hyde Park urban renewal project, was persuaded to pay $250,000 to CTS for Robie House and then present the house to the university. With the money, CTS bought the disused ZBT fraternity house next door, demolished it, and built there a useful dormitory christened Arthur Cushman McGiffert House. I have found that if one lives long enough, some of one's distinguished friends become buildings.

The university proceeded with adaptive reuses of the Robie House landmark and has reaped years of glamour and credit for saving a premier Chicago tourist attraction. It has now turned Robie House over to the Frank Lloyd Wright Foundation to operate.

ALTHOUGH creating a commission for conferring distinction on buildings was a good first step, the ultimate goal was to prevent destruction of landmarks. After the commission was created, we still had two significant battles, the fights to save Louis Sullivan's Schiller and Stock Exchange buildings.

Saving Robie House gave architectural preservationists a charge of confidence, but the next engagement was bitter. Adler and Sullivan's Schiller Building, which had been renamed the Garrick, stood at Dearborn and Randolph streets. Owners Balaban and Katz still operated the Woods Theater there, but the rest of the building had become almost empty. Balaban and Katz announced that because the theater was losing money, the building would be sold to a group that planned to demolish it and erect a parking garage.

The Schiller Building's facade, theater, and exquisite top-floor meeting hall were superlative Louis Sullivan creations. I am still haunted by their passing. The threat to destroy them resulted in the

largest public demonstrations to that date for architectural preservation. For weeks art and architecture students as well as interested
citizens engaged in daily picketing. Stauffer was there every day, and
so were celebrities whom he activated.

The media were generous in covering the demonstrations. The
classical music radio station WFMT, then a relatively new station,
dropped a prime-time program for a debate, in which I was a participant, on the Schiller Building. Stauffer stimulated Arnold Maremont,
a prominent, civic-minded businessman, to study saving the building
for downtown drama groups.

I introduced a city council resolution to save the building. As a
result of this action, arrangements were made for Maremont and a
group of aldermen to pay a visit and see for themselves. Representatives of Balaban and Katz showed us everything, including considerable debris and disorder backstage and upstairs. Despite all the fine
inner spaces and ornamentation, my fellow aldermen derided the
building and any prospect of saving it. Maremont commented, "I did
not know the theater stage was so small," and signaled withdrawal of
his interest.

Even so, the clamor about the demolition was so great that the
mayor used my city council resolution as a temporizing means to deny
a demolition permit. Balaban and Katz immediately filed suit, but, on
the basis of my pending resolution, the circuit court judge upheld the
mayor's position. The death of the Schiller Building was postponed.

Balaban and Katz appealed, and the city law department filed
briefs relying again on the "Despres resolution." Because there was
no enforceable architectural preservation law or ordinance, the appel-
late court did not take long to decide, and Sullivan's masterpiece was
destroyed. A few bas-reliefs of composers' heads from the facade
found their way to the front of Second City Theater on the North
Side. A repeated single Louis Sullivan design ornamented the parking garage on the Schiller site.

The Schiller Building became a memory, a collection of measurements and photographs. The lengthy campaign, in the long run, immeasurably strengthened Chicago's preservation organizations and raised public sentiment for retaining architectural landmarks.

The next public field test—also lost—involved Sullivan's Chicago Stock Exchange Building at the corner of LaSalle and Washington streets. It was a large structure functioning as an office building and could have been acquired by the city for governmental use. Unfortunately, a syndicate of predatory developers announced that they would replace it with a new office building.

The Stock Exchange Building was a great architectural wonder. The LaSalle Street facade and the second floor trading room were magnificent. The building lent itself to rehabilitation to meet the office needs of the city government, which was bursting out of City Hall across the street. Daley had the power but lacked the will to have the Public Building Commission acquire it and finance its rehabilitation. He could not resist the developers' drive or the lure of real estate taxes on a new office building.

Demonstrations, picketing, and adverse publicity met a stone wall in Daley. He did do something unusual, which indicated the pressure he felt. He personally held a one-man public hearing in the city council chambers, at which I tried to be persuasive. I could not change him. On the day the city council had to vote on the issue, some of the grim-faced developers came to the council chambers to make certain that their side would prevail. They need not have worried. The deal was secure. Soon demolition would begin.

The impending destruction was such a barbarous act that a concerned citizen, Alice DeCosta, was moved to donate more than a million dollars to save the trading room and reconstruct it in the Art Institute, where it can be seen today.

The need to photograph all the details of the building was so imperative that during the demolition period architectural photographer and determined preservationist Richard Nickel frequented the building with his camera until one day he was missing. The building had fallen and crushed him to death.

IN THE meantime, the commission had completed its work of "premiating" great buildings and held a dinner to honor its thirty-nine designated landmarks. This happy occasion was the only time that I received public recognition for a legislative achievement. What characterized many of my other legislative achievements was that I would introduce them, then fight for their enactment, and eventually see the administration or some of its aldermen reintroduce and pass them.

In the first edition of the valuable little book *Chicago's Famous Buildings*, Ira Bach, commissioner of planning, wrote, "On the basis of an ordinance drafted by Alderman Leon M. Despres, the 'Commission on Architectural Landmarks' was organized with seven members appointed by the Mayor and Daniel Catton Rich, then director of the Art Institute, as first chairman." In later editions, this mild credit was dropped.

DURING the interval, the Metropolitan Housing and Planning Council succeeded in having the Illinois Legislature pass a state law giving Chicago what no Illinois city had ever had, namely, the power to pass a landmark preservation ordinance. This action was under the 1870 Illinois Constitution, before the home rule for cities was established under the 1970 constitution. I promptly introduced a city council resolution for the passage of an ordinance, but nothing was done. This delay was strange because the Metropolitan Housing and Planning Council could not have obtained passage of the law in Springfield without approval by Daley's bloc. Thus, I had to assume that Daley had given his consent to the law and would presumably agree to an ordinance. Several times I tried to stimulate the city administration to introduce its ordinance, and finally, after a matter of years, the city administration did so. Naturally, no credit was given, and I made no public claim to any. I was thrilled to have achieved the goal of an enforceable public requirement for architectural preservation.

The ordinance, having been introduced by the administration, encountered no opposition and received speedy passage. Although I would have liked it to be stronger than it was, I was delighted that the city finally had an enforceable architectural and historical landmark preservation ordinance and commission. Many good commission appointments have been made, and years of excellent service to the city have not only preserved its architectural heritage but also stimulated public awareness and support for architectural preservation.

In 1983 Mayor Harold Washington appointed my wife, Marian, to the Commission on Architectural and Historical Landmarks. She served with distinction under three mayors before retiring in 2002.

The Rot of Political Patronage

9

Daley is the best we ever had for patronage.
I have 450 jobs.

Alderman Mathias "Paddy" Bauler, oral statement
to Despres around 1958

ONE DAY, the clerk of the council, with great enthusiasm, presented a congratulatory resolution. It warmly praised a city employee who was about to retire after forty-two years of service. The man had served as a "temp" for all those years. This meant he was appointed a temporary employee more than four decades earlier and had been reappointed successively every thirty or sixty days. Not once was he required to take a civil service examination. Now he was ready to retire. He was presented to the city council by the mayor as an exemplary employee. After his graceful speech, the aldermen responded with warm applause. Although Chicago was a city presumably governed by a civil service statute prescribing the manner of examination and the order of employment, at this time there were about eighty-five hundred other city employees who were temps.

When I ran for alderman against the Democratic Machine in 1955 and 1959, I faced an overwhelming patronage army of temporary employees recruited from all the offices controlled by the Democratic Party. These well-trained foot soldiers carried Machine candidates to victory after victory. This force with its superior numbers made it hard for any independent anywhere to win an election.

People were generally aware that political patronage existed and that one might get a job through a committeeman, alderman, or other local official. But most Chicagoans did not fully understand how the system worked and what a devastating effect it had.

At the head of the patronage system was the chairman of the Democratic Party of Cook County, Richard J. Daley. In 1953, Daley became chairman, and he remained in that position the rest of his life. It was his principal office, the one he had to attain in order to assume power countywide. But in order to protect his position as chairman, he needed to elect himself mayor. Daley realized that if someone else became mayor, that person might use his local power to turn out the chairman or to behave in office so that the chairman would have difficulty getting rid of him.

As chairman, Daley chose candidates and directed strategy for victory. He had at his disposal the patronage of each office that the party took over. He tightened his hold on patronage so that the temporary appointments were almost entirely within his control. Very little was left to individual officeholders' discretion. He had an effective system. At party headquarters, a careful record was kept of each political or temporary appointment, with the name of the committeeman charged with the temp. The party was organized under fifty ward committeemen for the city and thirty township committeemen for the rest of Cook County. Political jobs were apportioned among them partly in relation to their political need and greatly in proportion to their electoral results. Daley expected each committeeman to create and maintain a local political army and win at the polls.

The local committeeman could shape his force and have a temp fired if he did not produce results or please the committeeman, who would simply call the party office and ask that the temp be "vised." The person would be fired, and a substitute would be put on the public payroll.

Each committeeman was accountable for results. (I use the term "committeeman" because in Daley's reign he permitted only one female committeeperson in Chicago, and not for long.) Shortly before an election the chairman would have each committeeman see him personally and tell him the expected local election figures. Daley demanded accuracy. Woe to the committeeman who overstated or understated!

They were expected to bring in accurate figures. For inaccuracy they were disciplined, punished, or even removed. Daley was an efficient chairman.

Each committeeman always wanted more political appointments, and Daley obliged. By conquering one office after another, Daley had more patronage at the party's disposal than ever before in the city's history. In Daley's Eleventh Ward, where he himself was ward committeeman, he had, according to reporter Ed Schreiber of the *Tribune*, twenty-two hundred temporary jobs at his disposal. When new jobs became available, the central office of the party would distribute them.

Lynn Williams, the New Trier committeeman, once told me that Daley's party secretary had recently phoned him to say, "We have two ranger jobs in the forest preserves. Let us know whom you want to place in them."

Patronage was something the party and the committeemen did not discuss in public. It was a little tarnished, like prostitution. Paddy Bauler's avowal and Lynn Williams's report to me were rare explicit admissions. At a budget hearing, I persistently questioned the commissioner of Streets and Sanitation on his three thousand temps.

"Weren't these patronage employees designated by the party?" I asked.

"No, Alderman," he answered firmly. "We hire the best people we can find."

Mayor Martin Kennelly, whom Daley toppled in 1955, had determined, with business support, to extend civil service to all nonexecutive employees. As a result, when Daley was elected, he found only two thousand temps on the city payroll.

The rest of the employees were tenured civil service workers who were not subject to being fired for poor political performance. This was definitely not conducive to future Democratic Party victories. Daley needed and wanted more party patronage.

Kennelly had appointed a diligent chairman of the Civil Service Commission, who was determined to prevent corrupt civil service examinations and the kind of leakage of examination questions that had occurred in the past. Unfortunately, the man whom the mayor selected died in office and the questions for the next police patrolman's exam were found in his safe deposit box. Apparently, the chairman lacked confidence in the commission's tenured secretary and felt that the only safe place for the test was his own safe deposit box. He was right, but the law said that the questions had been compromised, and the entire examination was canceled.

Chairman Daley believed his urgent task as mayor was to tackle the civil service scene. He immediately increased the number of temps. In his mind, the party needed many more than the two thousand for its election battles. In Milwaukee, less than ninety miles away from Chicago's city hall, the number of temporary employees was between eighty and ninety.

Mayor Daley appointed a new chairwoman for the Civil Service Commission, one who set about adjusting the situation. Scheduled examinations were canceled. The posting of lists of successful candidates was postponed unconscionably. New examinations were abandoned. The civil service program was directed toward diminishing civil service. In his tenure as mayor, Chairman Daley was able to increase the number of city temps to more than eighty-five hundred.

A professional employee of the Civil Service Commission came to Alderman Einar Johnson and me after I had been alderman about six months with the story of what was happening at the Civil Service Commission. It was frightful. We introduced a resolution in the city council and had a hearing at which we interrogated the new civil service chairwoman. She was flustered by my questions, and angry. From her viewpoint, she was simply following instructions and could not see why aldermen were holding her to account for what the chief executive was telling her to do.

It took observation of city government over a long time for me to understand the full effect this partisan patronage had on city government. The temps viewed the party as their true employer. They realized they had been hired by a committeeman, were protected in their jobs by him, and could be vised by the same individual at any time for any reason or for none. Consequently, the individual lived under the lash of patronage and felt almost immune from his or her superior on the job. City Treasurer Morris Sachs observed that, if one employee out of thirty-five can get along without working, the example is not lost on the other thirty-four. Promotions, transfers, and standards were subject to partisan political influence. The city government did not fall. Rather, the quality of city government was impaired. As mayor, Daley was interested in running the city. As chairman, he wanted patronage to win elections. Was this a conflict of interest? Decidedly so. The quality of work for the city deteriorated as the Machine became more and more efficient.

In a few operations, Daley demanded exceptional performance, such as snow removal. There, his power over temporary employees whom he could threaten with immediate termination was important in exacting superior work. Generally, in actual practice, if the temp successfully delivered the vote in his precinct or performed the work the committeeman assigned him, the job was secure. If not, he was vised. There was no Civil Service Commission or process to which he could appeal.

The Democratic Machine was not interested in allocating any patronage to me. On my part, if I had asked for and obtained it, I would have been a hostage to the Machine. Then, if I had opposed the Machine, my temps would have been vised and I would have been beleaguered.

It took me a good period of time to see that partisan patronage was a hemorrhage of city energy. It was an embezzlement of public funds for the benefit of an election army. In my first year or two I had tried to find individual defects in the budget, such as overspending or ghost payrolling. Unfortunately, to do this, I lacked an investigative staff. If I found a budget appropriation that seemed excessive and if some of the other aldermen and I introduced resolutions to reduce it, the administration would brief aldermen to recite what the employees in question actually did or could be expected to do. They would then posture as if to ridicule me for trying to eliminate some vital city service.

"Are you trying to destroy the alcoholic treatment center, Alderman?" they might ask. Finally I realized that the great defect in Chicago government operations was the patronage system itself. I prepared a careful but dramatic memorandum detailing the extent of partisan appointments in city employment. It carefully estimated the annual waste at $40 million, detailed the impairment of city government, and used those facts as the basis for criticism of the budget.

Through the media, at public meetings, in campaign talks, I was able to repeat the story dramatically. I did so whenever I was asked to talk about city government in Chicago. It always seemed fresh to the audience because there was no general understanding of what Chicago's partisan political patronage meant.

The city had a long tradition that a job could be obtained through an alderman. As a result, during my entire twenty years in that position, people came to me seeking help in finding employment and expecting that I could write a letter and get them a job. I had to find substitute ways of leading people to work opportunities. I would explain that I had no patronage jobs, but that I would do what I could to direct them to work.

Through a supporter who worked at United States Steel, for example, I was able for some years to send people to the employment office there. If they qualified, they were hired. United States Steel was constantly hiring, and those I sent were given immediate examinations to test their ability and quality. If they became steelworkers, however, I had neither the desire nor the ability to vise them, as a committeeman would have had if they held city temp jobs. Another

method I used was to collect notices of impending civil service examinations and turn them over to constituents as possible sources of
employment. I could let them know in particular when the next
firefighters' or police examination was to be given because those
were not subject to temporary appointment.

When people seemed doubtful about their own capacities, I would
refer them to Jewish Vocational Service. I would tell them that even
though the title was "Jewish," the agency was open to everyone and
was, so far as I knew, the best employment agency for steering people to jobs they could perform. This was, of course, not as effective
as a committeeman's sending people directly to enrollment on the
public payroll.

During my twenty years as alderman I saw the sharp rise and the
beginning of the fall of partisan political patronage. I saw Chairman
Daley take power as mayor and build the city's total temps from two
thousand to eighty-five hundred. Similar increases occurred in other
party-dominated government units, such as the county of Cook, the
Sanitary District of Chicago, the forest preserves, the Chicago park
system, the Municipal Tuberculosis Sanitarium, the Alcoholic Treatment Center, and so on. Then I saw the effect of the U.S. Supreme
Court's 1972 *Shakman* decisions that political hiring, firing, and
treatment of nonexecutive public employees were unconstitutional.
The days of a chairman's enormous power with thirty-five thousand
party jobs in his hands from dozens of offices are gone. There are
other methods of city patronage. Officeholders still have temporary
executive appointments. They can still award lucrative contracts
to political supporters. But the almost totalitarian control of the
municipality through patronage employees is no longer legal.

Getting Reelected

An Even Tougher Battle

10

Is Alderman Leon Despres (5th) in trouble in his home ward?

Political reporter Charles Cleveland,
Chicago Daily News, October 18, 1958

The 1959 election for my second term was not an ordinary battle. Rather, for me, it seemed more a convulsion. After it was over, my wife, Marian, said she could "never go through anything like that again." I took that to mean she was vetoing my third term, but the 1963 election would be a breeze, as would be those in 1967 and 1971.

Until September 1958, my first aldermanic term had proved satisfactory to my constituents and seemed to promise an easy reelection to a second term. Then the roof fell in. I had shown myself dependable, conscientious about the ward's needs, opposed to corruption, in favor of civil rights, friendly with the university, supportive of Hyde Park–Kenwood urban renewal, and able to obtain new street lights. I had pushed through an ordinance that took away aldermanic extortion for driveway permits, obtained a novel architectural preservation measure, and properly assailed the excesses of patronage and the budget. Like Gilbert and Sullivan's major general, "I was the very model of a model" Fifth Ward alderman, looking as though I would be hard to beat for reelection.

There was just one troublesome item. Although supportive of urban renewal, I had raised a nagging question: "What kind of urban renewal?"

In 1956, there had been a first, small urban renewal plan. It had displaced a few residents, eliminated a lot of old saloons, pushed out actors Nichols and May from their storefront, and produced middle-income housing as well as a shopping center. Then planning began for much bigger urban renewal from Forty-seventh to Fifty-ninth streets between Cottage Grove Avenue and the Illinois Central Railroad. The area covered nearly two square miles.

This urban renewal plan was as troublesome an issue as I had ever faced. Being in favor of it brought me support from the university's administration, business interests, and constituents who wanted to keep the community attractive. But being in favor of it also brought anger from whole blocks of constituents and businesses who faced demolition and removal. It created hostility among constituents in Woodlawn who believed the University of Chicago was about to annex their neighborhood. The Catholic Archdiocese published a strong statement on the unfairness of expelling the poor and not providing them with affordable housing.

Although financial compensation was available for the displaced, this did not satisfy either my critics or my conscience. Most of the sufferers were poor, black, or both. They and their philosophical defenders kept telling me that the urban renewal plan would eliminate affordable housing and build only expensive housing.

The University of Chicago administration, which had contractual control of planning, had not taken me into the planning process. A technical expert, Jack Meltzer, had charge of that work, and a resourceful university administrator, Julian Levi, carried out university administration policy while inventing some of his own. At times Meltzer and Levi showed me what they had done after they did it. At other times they met privately with objecting businesses, property owners, or community institutions to negotiate changes, but they did not invite me. I was treated as the alderman who had no choice but to vote "Aye." I had no opportunity to shape what was coming, except once, to gain a parking lot for the University National Bank, which was being treated shamelessly.

At last, the city council committee hearings on the plan were set for a day in September 1958. During all the preceding week, preparations had gone forward for the presentation of impressive evidence and exhibits, but the alderman was being allowed no part in them. In the city council chambers, where the committee hearings were to take place, I saw municipal employees hanging huge banners, graphics, and photographs I had never seen.

On the Saturday before the city council committee hearing, I had lunch at the Quadrangle Club with a young Tory English lord, whom the International Visitors Center sent to me to "meet a Chicago alderman." He was the chairman of the House of Lords committee on housing and asked me about the urban renewal plan. When I told him about the displacement of poor residents and the almost total failure to provide any low-cost replacement, he said unhesitatingly, "That's a cheat."

"That's a cheat" galvanized me. I asked myself whether I, a liberal Chicago alderman, was acquiescing in an arrangement that a Tory English lord unhesitatingly saw as a cheat. I decided I had to speak up. I could not let urban renewal go on without an effort to bring about fair play. Over the weekend, I ruminated over "It's a cheat" and felt more and more determined. My wife, Marian, was away, and I ruminated alone.

On Monday, my objections were ready to explode. At the city council hearing they did just that. I felt that the plan was speeding past me and that unless I spoke out at this juncture, I would be forever approving what an English Tory lord had called a cheat. I was thinking not especially in terms of the plan's racial implications but rather of its economic unfairness—tearing down a lot of low-cost housing and not providing any reasonable economic way for the people displaced by urban renewal to reenter the community. The plan did include a few public housing apartment buildings at the very edge of the urban renewal area. These were inside the segregated ghetto.

The hearing started with a procession of supporting witnesses, and I began asking each one, "Why is there no adequate provision for low-income public housing?"

The words were like a thunderclap in the hearing chamber. What? Despres, the alderman of the ward, was tearing into the urban renewal plan, "attacking" University of Chicago chancellor Kimpton, "offending" female professor Soia Mentschikoff, "badgering" witnesses, and endangering the whole Hyde Park–Kenwood urban renewal effort?

At the noon recess I explained to reporters I was not attacking the plan, just trying to make it fair, but my explanations were in vain. The big news stories on the hearing were about Despres's relentless attacks on urban renewal.

At the same time, some people rushed up to congratulate me. I sensed immediately that I had riven my old dependable base of support and had possibly started to acquire a new one. I was aware at once that I had put my reelection in jeopardy. Mark Twain wrote, "Always do right. It will gratify some people and astonish the rest," but I was deeply unsure whether what I gained would make up for what I had just thrown aside.

FOR MY rash behavior, I expected from my close supporters only reproaches. The next morning, I, as usual, entered Dick Meyer's car to ride downtown. He was then my closest and wisest adviser. I awaited a barrage of criticism, but he said, "You have made public housing the issue in your next election, and I can't think of a better one to run on." I was comforted and strengthened, but I remained anxious and worried continuously until the election finally took place in late February.

The election campaign battle lines were drawn at once. The conservative property owners were furious at me and terrified that, if I were reelected, I would kill urban renewal. The administration of the University of Chicago, our ward's largest employer and property owner, felt the same.

The Fifth Ward Democratic Machine was neither furious nor terrified. It was delighted. Committeeman Barnet Hodes exulted. I seemed to him to have shot myself in the foot and, by doing so, enabled him to form an alliance of his precinct army with some University of Chicago personnel to elect a candidate of his choice. He had always yearned for such a respectable arrangement.

A few of my supporters were dazed by my abruptness at the city council hearing, but some were dazzled, and others just liked me as alderman. New supporters came from among critics of the urban renewal plan, and especially from blacks. They sensed more quickly than I had that the dominant factor by far in the public housing fight was race and not class, as I then thought.

Until the February election, though, my anxieties persisted. My main campaign task was to justify my championship of public housing in urban renewal and, by showing that I really supported community improvement, to win back the homeowners and residents whom I had terrified.

Immediately, under Julian Levi's leadership, an energetic anti-Despres committee was formed, including faculty members Walter Blum and others. They were indefatigable and effective in alienating almost the entire faculties of law, medicine, and business from me. I could not sway them, but the humanities faculties were with me.

Levi soon met with Barnet Hodes, the Democratic ward committeeman, and promised to provide university community resources, newspaper editorial support, and individual financial backing for a candidate against me. In 1959, newspaper editorials were still crucial. That was before the saturating influence of television.

Levi's offer of support led Hodes into overconfidence and into making a political misstep for which I have always been grateful. Foreseeing an easy victory, Hodes designated his nephew, Allen Dropkin, as the Machine-selected candidate. Dropkin was and is an able lawyer, but he was not then politically experienced. Levi and his committee accepted Hodes's choice and worked hard to fulfill their commitments. To them, a Machine alderman inclined to obey his uncle-committeeman was preferable to me.

Hodes always spoke disingenuously about having designated his nephew. "His being my nephew had nothing to do with it," he would say. "What happened was that Joe Pinkert and a committee came to me and said that they had a fine candidate and asked me to run Allen Dropkin. Because of that, I decided I too would support him."

In the 1955 campaign, the Hodes forces had not begun to slander me compared with what they would do in 1959. In one precinct they would say I was a homosexual and in another that I was an adulterer. In one precinct they said that I attended mass as a Catholic and in another that I had an illegitimate child. In most of the Hyde Park precincts they could just refer to what I did at the urban renewal hearings. They gave people the impression I had attacked Chancellor Kimpton and endangered all urban renewal.

At nearly all meetings and every coffee, I had to answer hostile questions. I learned not to seem irritated, to refrain from anger, and to be careful not to raise my voice in indignation. I had to persuade people about the beauties of scattered-site public housing and my strong support of fair urban renewal.

The hubbub I had raised about unfairness in the Hyde Park–Kenwood urban renewal reflected public discontent so strongly that Daley alderman John Egan approached me and asked if I would be satisfied if the renewal plan would include 180 units of low-rise scattered public housing. I could hardly conceal my delight. Egan spoke for Daley, and the 180 units were included in the plan. I had hoped for more, but that helped me with my supporters, although not much with my enemies.

The Hodes precinct forces worked hard, and in some precincts, they were unbeatable. They had eight or ten capable Jewish captains in Hyde Park and Woodlawn, all nonresidents but one. They had been trained in Jack Arvey's West-Side Twenty-fourth Ward, where precinct work was a nonstop operation. They had a few invincible, non-Jewish, white and black captains in Woodlawn. Fighting them for the hearts and minds of voters was hard political work, and the best our volunteers could do against some of them was to whittle away at their majority.

Our ward had a few good Republican precinct captains and some considerably less able ones. All but one or two stayed on our side. The university administration tried to win over Bunny East, the Republican committeeman, and almost succeeded.

Our winning strength was in our volunteers. Louis Silverman again managed the campaign with the same flashes of genius he had displayed in 1955.

At times I felt discouraged and almost ready to quit. On one such occasion, Ab Mikva bucked me up and told me that the Hodes-Dropkin camp was also thinking about quitting. Neither of us did. On our side, we were getting information and even some marginal help from a few regular Democrats eager to topple Hodes.

We never had enough money. On top of everything else we had to raise funds to pay Silverman's salary, who was on leave from his firm. We also had to collect funds for the Republican captains' expenses for election day. There were always new demands.

Politically, I never worked so hard. There were endless meetings, coffees, Sunday morning get-togethers, and handshaking sorties. I had to keep myself under control. I had to overcome disappointment at defections—friends around the university community who supported the other side.

The *Chicago Daily News* faltered, and I had to spend time assuring its editorial writers that I deserved support. Levi, keeping his promise to Hodes, had organized influence on the daily newspaper publishers to support Dropkin. Although besieged by him, the editorial writer at the *Daily News* remained strong and independent. Finally, against the publisher's orders, he supported me and, after the election, had to retire.

As the fervor of the campaign mounted, we saw that we were making gradual progress. My endless explanations took effect. So did Allen Dropkin's lack of political experience. His backers began sending substitutes to speak for him. I would then present my views vigorously and ignore comments from the Dropkin replacements. At an evening meeting of the League of Women Voters in Mandel Hall to which the candidates were invited, more than 650 people showed up to listen to the debate, more than would appear today.

In his main talk, Dropkin spoke adequately, but he killed himself in the question period. When asked his position on any subject, he answered, "I would have to study the question carefully and then reach a decision on it." When he gave the same answer a third time to a third question about issues, the audience laughed. When asked what committee he would like to be on, he answered that he would consult his supporters and decide. He lost votes.

We had a television appearance, on a Sunday morning *City Desk* half hour, and here he was also indecisive. I was astonished at how many people saw the TV program and spoke to me favorably about it. This should have given me a notion of the mighty political power of television we have come to know.

Why was Hodes so shortsighted as to choose Dropkin? It was not only because of his self-confidence after Levi offered him so many political goodies but also for another reason dating from Alderman Bob Merriam's time. Hodes figured that if he elected another Merriam-type candidate, he would have a hollow victory. It would have been politically fruitless. Hodes wanted an alderman who would always call him uncle, and that was his nephew.

As election day approached, Committeeman Hodes realized he needed help. The Democratic Machine downtown asked all ward organizations to assist the Fifth Ward organization in any way they could. Friends of ours in other parts of the city told us with alarm about this citywide appeal.

On loan from other organizations, precinct workers came to Hodes's help, but they met resistance from the voters. Hodes raised all the money he wanted, but, as Republican committeeman Bunny East said, "Money can only get you so far."

On the Sunday before the election, we had the biggest Despres meeting in my experience, about six hundred or seven hundred volunteers, at International House. We had never had so many solid workers in any campaign. I was buoyed, but still worried.

On election day, Klaus Ollendorff drove me around. I followed the usual course—visiting each polling place, encouraging our workers, greeting the judges, and leaving a bag of Peerless candy furnished by Bob Picken. Just getting in and out of the car, walking into the polling places, and going back to the car wore out two more drivers and certainly the candidate. I was heartened by our forces, discouraged where the enemy was strong, and finally I was just exhausted.

At home, I fell into a deep sleep. I awoke to take a hot bath. I feared I had lost. While I was in the tub, Marian took a telephone message and called to me repeatedly, "You have won by thirteen hundred votes." I felt depressed. Imagine—last time I had won by thirty-seven hundred votes!

"Get up and get dressed," she said, "there's a crowd of enthusiastic workers just waiting for you to come."

I rallied, understanding what a great victory it was for everyone who took part in the campaign. The adversaries had thrown everything they had into the race, and lost. So winning by thirteen hundred votes was a far greater achievement than winning by thirty-seven hundred votes had been four years earlier.

A few months later, Senator Paul Douglas told me, "I think you can be sure that the Democratic organization will not oppose you again." He was right.

The victory celebration was exhilarating. Before it was all over, Marshall Korshak of the Hodes organization came over to congratulate us, and the newspapers published only that photo! Soon afterward, the defeated Hodes stepped down as ward committeeman, and Korshak replaced him. We had been shooting politically for alderman, but one of our shots hit the ward committeeman, and he did not survive.

Sparring with Daley

11

*Whereas, the present park system of the City of Chicago
has been and now is a great blessing to our citizens in
giving them fresh air and sunshine which is so difficult to
obtain in a crowded and growing city . . ."*

Chicago City Council resolution, November 6, 1899

MAYOR DALEY was almost always courteous toward me. He was so
by training. Besides, politically, why should he not be? For twenty
years, he always had the votes to turn down any proposal I made. But
on May 20, 1970, he completely lost his composure and his temper.
Looking at me, he hurled a withering epithet: "Liar," he exploded.

"Liar" was a word he had never used in the city council before
then and never did again. What was it that shook his confidence and
made him lose his equilibrium?

The administration had presented an ordinance to give up 3.6
acres of park land in Washington Park for the construction of a
school. From a lifetime of experience with Jackson and Washington
parks, I know how vital parks are to a big city that does not have
enough park space. I also know how prone public officials are to use
park land for schools, convention halls, parking lots, and sanitori-
ums because park land costs nothing and can be taken. The first taking of a park land site for a nonpark purpose is usually followed by
expansion. We soon hear:

"We need more space for exhibitions."

"We need space for an electrical installation."

"We definitely need a parking lot."

And the original taking expands until, like the proverbial camel, it upsets the whole plan for park use.

In the brief debate over the ordinance to take away part of Washington Park, I was about to quote the opinion of a society of architects sent to the city's Department of Planning, insisting that park land should not be used for nonpark purposes. I was barely into my first minute of debate, let alone the other nine minutes the rules entitled me to, when I said that taking land away from Washington Park was a murder of the park. At this, the mayor exploded with "Liar."

"You are twisting this as you usually do," the mayor continued with lack of grace. I remembered that Mayor Edward Kelly (1933–47) used to descend from the rostrum and engage in heated debate with the aldermen. I knew that *Robert's Rules of Order* required the chairman to desist from debate unless willing to assume the floor. I decided to remind the mayor of this.

"If you want to debate this," I suggested, "you should leave the chair."

Northwest Side alderman Seymour Simon supported me and said that if Mayor Daley did indeed want to debate me, he should step down from the rostrum and proceed.

In his heat of passion, the mayor did not, could not, resist the challenge.

"I'll tell anyone at any time that they are lying if they are lying," he sputtered. "And I'll take the floor to do it."

It is difficult to find a figure of speech strong enough to dramatize the apparent difference in the political power then attributed to the two of us. Daley had total control of more than 90 percent of the votes. He had been accurately described as "the most powerful local politician in American history." What shook him was the realization that there is more to power than the won-lost columns indicate. He was up against public opinion. He handed the gavel to Alderman Claude W. B. Holman, the designated president pro-tem of the city council, and descended to the floor, ready to argue his position and excoriate his critics.

The *Chicago Tribune* reported the next day:

> Mayor Daley, in an unprecedented move, left the rostrum at yesterday's council meeting with the announced intent of debating Alderman Leon M. Despres (Fifth) and calling him a liar.
>
> But he never did become involved in the floor debate with Despres because Alderman Claude W. B. Holman (Fourth), Council Pro-Tem who replaced Daley as presiding officer, failed to recognize the Mayor.
>
> Explained Holman, "Well, the Mayor didn't rise to seek recognition."

Both Mayor Daley and Alderman Holman thought better of their proposed floor debate.

I Get Shot

Next time, take a cab.

Saul Alinsky

12

REPORTS OF violence in the streets, hold-ups, and beatings were especially frustrating because there was so little an alderman could do. While I might press the police for additional protection and more police officers on the beat, the violence comes from deep causes beyond the power of an individual alderman. I did what I could and got help from the community.

The Southeast Chicago Commission, an organization sponsored by the community and the University of Chicago, provided a lot of help. It had a full-time criminologist who kept in constant contact with the police to beef up security and follow through on enforcement.

A special outrage arose when an older woman was beaten up in daytime on Cornell Avenue near Fifty-sixth Street. Despite this and other crimes, I stated that the neighborhood was really safer than it seemed, and I urged constituents not to give in to fear of violence.

Soon after, I had a test of my reassurances. On December 26, 1967, a few weeks before my sixtieth birthday, I stayed late in my downtown law office and arrived in Hyde Park shortly after ten o'clock to pick up my aldermanic correspondence. The office was then on Fifty-fifth Street at Cornell Avenue. As I locked the door to go home, a CTA bus went by, and I knew that none would be coming for some time. Then a Yellow Cab went by. I had missed both of them.

It was a beautiful warm evening, and I walked west on Fifty-fifth Street to go home. At Blackstone Avenue, I saw three boys on the other side of the street. As I walked a little farther, I noticed that they had crossed toward me and had begun quickly following me. I knew they would soon overtake me on the dark sidewalk, so to avoid them I stepped into the bright street. There were fluorescent streetlights, and usually there was steady motor traffic. I planned to stop a car, because that would disperse the three boys.

But that night, there was no traffic at all. And when I turned around I saw that the three had also stepped into the street about twenty feet away. One of them was pointing a gun at me. I threw myself into the street and wrapped my head around the front tire of an automobile just as I heard a second boy say, "Burn him." A shot hit my right thigh. Amazingly, there was no pain. I thought, "This is it," and hoped they were satisfied.

To my surprise, a second shot hit my left knee. I felt I must let them know that they had hit me and I uttered a terrible scream as if in frightful pain and then kept shouting for help as loud as I could. The boys began running as people started appearing.

Since my leg had been hit, I knew it would not be wise for me to stand. As people poured out of the townhouses and the big University Apartments, someone carefully took hold of me and dragged or carried me to the entrance of one of the townhouses to await an ambulance. Just then a man with a beard appeared, saw my leg was bleeding, and said, "I am a physician. May I slit your trouser leg?" I was in no state to say no.

"You are all right. You have not been hit in your artery," he told me. I was deeply grateful to him.

"What is your name?" I asked. He declined. Later, my aunt asked if he had a beard. He did. She concluded he must have been a divine messenger. Soon an ambulance took me to the University of Chicago Hospital. To my amazement, when we reached the hospital for surgery, the area was filled with reporters. Also, my wife was there. I still do not understand how they all got there so quickly.

Next morning the *Tribune*'s headline was "Ald. Despres Shot

Twice." Although telephone calls would normally have been denied me, the first thing next morning I had one from Mayor Daley. He did not want one of his aldermen to be shot, even an opposition one. He was warmly consoling and said that now we have to take steps to regulate guns and hope we will be successful.

While the telephone line was still open, a call came from Saul Alinsky, an expert community organizer and a friend. I asked him what advice he could give me, and he said, "Next time, take a cab. And keep using the crutches as long as you can."

The experience and the publicity brought a flood of messages, calls, cards, warm letters, books, and endless expressions of support and sympathy, which were surprising and very consoling. After a couple of weeks, I was still on crutches but back at office work and at the city council. On March 21, the first day of spring, I was able to ride a bicycle again.

I reevaluated safety in the streets in Hyde Park. I stopped walking alone at night.

Were the boys ever caught? Yes, in about four weeks. They were ages twelve, sixteen, and seventeen. The one who had fired the handgun was twelve years old. He remained in juvenile detention until he was twenty-one. The others were convicted and imprisoned for robberies committed that night. The gun, which they had "rented" for the day, was never recovered. The police believed that one boy's father, who worked at Inland Steel, had thrown it into a mass of molten metal.

Samuel and Henrietta Despres, Leon's parents, in 1903,
the year of their marriage
Author's collection

Leon Despres, February 2, 1910
Author's collection

Leon in 1918, Pentwater, Michigan
Author's collection

Family passport photo, 1922
Author's collection

Leon Despres (right), accompanied by noted French writer and existentialist Jean-Paul Sartre (center), walks down a Chicago alley with a trade unionist. The visit was in 1948 or 1949, before Leon's election as an alderman.
Author's collection

Pre–city council civic involvement: Leon holds the symbol for the co-op movement at the 1952 groundbreaking for the Pioneer co-op apartments at 5427 S. Dorchester Avenue in Hyde Park.

A boy campaigns for Robert Merriam for mayor and Leon Despres for
Fifth Ward alderman in the 1955 election.
Chicago Historical Society (ICHi-37807)

Aldermanic candidate Leon Despres
and mayoral candidate Robert Merriam
Chicago Historical Society (ICHi-37798)

Aldermanic candidate Despres in
his first election campaign performs
the traditional baby-kissing ritual
while the child demonstrates the
normal reluctance.
Chicago Historical Society (ICHi-37806)

Leon and his wife, Marian, celebrate his victory in the 1959 aldermanic election.
Chicago Historical Society (ICHi-37808)

Newly elected alderman Leon Despres and Senator Paul Douglas, a friend, supporter, and former Fifth Ward alderman, attend the Independent Voters of Illinois dinner after the election. H. A. Marin Photography, Chicago Historical Society (ICHi-37811)

Alderman Despres shares a moment in the city council chambers with Alderman Mathias "Paddy" Bauler. Albert C. Flores, Chicago Historical Society (ICHi-37809)

A mobile office in a truck and a boy with a meet-the-alderman sign demonstrate one of Despres's many efforts to reach out to the Hyde Park and Woodlawn communities during his first term in the city council.
Chicago Historical Society (ICHi-37812)

Leon Despres in his law office in 1960
Author's collection

The Frank Lloyd Wright–designed Robie House in Hyde Park is an international architectural treasure. Alderman Despres initiated the successful protest that saved the building from the wrecking ball.

Photograph by Richard Nickel, courtesy of the Richard Nickel Committee, Chicago, Illinois

The Stock Exchange Building represents a failed preservation effort in which Alderman Despres was involved. Not only was the building destroyed but it took the life of photographer Richard Nickel as his camera recorded the destruction.

Photograph by Richard Nickel, courtesy of the Richard Nickel Committee, Chicago, Illinois

The delicate, magnificent beauty of the proscenium in Adler and Sullivan's Garrick Theater
Photograph by Richard Nickel, courtesy of the Richard Nickel Committee, Chicago, Illinois

Despite preservation efforts and a temporarily successful bill in city council introduced by Alderman Despres, the Garrick Theatre was not saved.
Photograph by Richard Nickel, courtesy of the Richard Nickel Committee, Chicago, Illinois

With civil rights activist Dick Gregory (left) and Ed Reddick (right), Alderman Despres leads a march in the early 1960s to demand that Chicago public school libraries put more books about African Americans on their shelves.
Chicago Historical Society (ICHi-34757)

The Fifth Ward alderman joins a 1963 sit-in at the Chicago Board of Education offices at 228 N. LaSalle Street to protest segregation in city schools and to call for redistricting to alleviate it.

Legendary Chicago reporter and commentator Lu Palmer interviews
Alderman Despres in the mid-1960s.
Chicago Historical Society (ICHi-37810)

Leon Despres campaigning by phone
Chicago Historical Society (ICHi-37813)

Marian Despres, Alderman
Despres—recovering from being
shot—and their daughter,
Linda Baskin, leave the council
chambers in 1968.
Copyright © *Chicago Sun-Times*,
reprinted by permission

Despres (left), National
Farmers Union president James
Patton (second from left), and
segregationist Alabama governor
George Wallace (third from left)
appear with Irv Kupcinet on his
television show in 1968.
Chicago Historical Society
(ICHi-37797)

Alderman Despres arrives at a city council meeting by bicycle in 1970, participating in a boycott of the Chicago Transit Authority over planned fare hikes.

Susan Catania and Susan Davis accompany Alderman Despres during the
Grant Park Coalition for Jobs March in 1973.
Chicago Historical Society (ICHi-37799)

Mayor Jane Byrne and city council parliamentarian Leon Despres shake
hands as she steps down as mayor in 1983. He stayed on in his position under
Mayor Harold Washington.
Chicago Historical Society, Despres collection (ICHi-37796)

Leon Despres participates in the groundbreaking ceremony for
Harper Square Child Center at 4800 S. Lake Park Avenue.
Author's collection

Leon and Marian Despres with Mayor Harold Washington in the mid-1980s.
At the time, Marian served on the Commission on Chicago Landmarks.
Chicago Historical Society (ICHi-35559)

Alderman Despres, who had personally known Clarence Darrow, speaks at the
1992 memorial ceremony held in the noted attorney's honor each year on the bridge
that leads to Wooded Island in Jackson Park.
Author's collection

Our City's Basic Problem

13

*In terms of racial residential patterns, Chicago is the
most segregated city of more than 500,000 in the country.*

United States Civil Rights Commission, 1959

"I'VE BEEN thinking about all our plans for Chicago," Al Olglobin,
a bright, young city-planning expert, told me when we happened to
meet downtown in late 1959. He had been hired by Chicago Plan
Commissioner Ira Bach "to do some thinking about planning for
Chicago."

What he said next abruptly changed the focus of my political career.

"I have come to the conclusion," he said, "that the city's most
important problem is racial segregation. It blocks all our plans."

Work on that problem would—from that moment on—become
my primary aldermanic job.

Racial discrimination, I had long been aware, hurts members of
the minority groups against whom it is aimed. I had not seen, though,
that it blocks nearly all plans to improve and develop the whole city.
For example, whites would oppose nonghetto housing projects
financed by public funds because they would bring in blacks. Blacks
would oppose ghetto improvements because they said "Urban renewal
means Negro removal." The result was stasis.

Olglobin's words hit me. He was a planner, not an advocate as
I was. What he said suddenly illuminated all my experiences in
Chicago city government. From then on, the struggle to end racial
discrimination topped my aldermanic goals and shaped my public

and private life. When I first became alderman, I had set five priority areas of concentration:

1. City planning
2. Civil rights and racial equality
3. Government efficiency and honesty
4. Housing and urban renewal
5. Responsiveness to local ward problems

Although unexpected crises and special problems, such as a 1960 police burglary scandal, would suddenly claim my aldermanic attention, my five priorities remained for twenty years. Only, after my talk with Olglobin, numbers 1 and 2 changed places. From then on, I knew my most important contribution would be to respond as effectively as I could to the racial discrimination that was hurting our city. It touched my deepest concerns.

My first aldermanic experience with the Daley administration's racial housing policy had come only a few weeks after the 1955 election, at my first meeting of the City Council Housing and Planning Committee. On the agenda was an ordinance for federally funded middle-income housing in an all-white neighborhood near Eighty-seventh Street and Western Avenue.

Because of the neighborhood's fear that this would bring in non-white residents, the housing project had been a major 1955 election issue for the Daley-supported alderman. Now, at a city council meeting, Mayor Daley's representative was preparing to make good the candidate's promise to junk the project.

A crowd of residents was present. The committee was addressed by James Downes, a real estate consultant who was the mayor's "housing coordinator."

"We are withdrawing this ordinance temporarily to restudy it," he said. "We are definitely not doing so permanently, but we want to go over it carefully." I did not believe him.

I then naïvely thought that any alderman who was African American, even one who supported Daley, would be an ally on civil rights issues, and I whispered to Second Ward alderman William Harvey, "We know the real reason why he is doing this."

Harvey smiled and whispered back, "We have to support the mayor."

That was my first moment of truth about Daley's black aldermen. In their personal experiences, each of them knew much more about racial discrimination than I. In their hearts they knew what needed to be done. What I then failed to understand was that all the Daley black aldermen were making a living off politics. Despite twinges, they were under the domination of two bosses, Second Ward committeeman William Dawson and Democratic Party chairman Richard J. Daley. The black aldermen had to support the two men who controlled their comfortable livelihoods. Only long, long after this did one of them, Ralph Metcalfe, give way to constituents' pressure for civil rights and declare his independence of Daley's racial policies.

Downes's temporary withdrawal of the housing ordinance was, in truth, forever. Years later, they did find a new use for the land— Quigley Catholic Seminary South—to which no white racist could object, even though Quigley might train a black seminarian. Bigotry won, integrated middle-income housing lost, and I gained insight.

Soon afterward, I involved myself in the aftermath of the murder of Emmett Till. He was a gangly, stuttering, black adolescent from the Englewood neighborhood who was visiting relatives in Mississippi. In a store there, some white men thought he ogled or leered at a white female. The next day he was found in a stream, dead and weighted down by stones.

My good, good friend Willard Saxby Townsend, who was then gravely ill, called me. "I want you to do something so the Dawson outfit can never beat you. You have to think of something to do about Emmett Till." Bill Townsend was an extraordinary person. He was university educated, but because he was black, he could find work only as a redcap carrying bags for passengers at Chicago's NorthWestern Station. He organized the redcaps nationally and became the first African American to sit on the executive board of the Congress of Industrial Organizations (CIO). As a lawyer, I had represented the redcaps' union since June 1937.

His concern deeply touched me. Far better than I, he understood, and was trying to help me do so, that an aldermanic record of mere goodwill could leave me vulnerable to attack among black voters. They might see me as just a condescending white and not a champion. He was telling me, "You have to be a genuine active advocate. You have to be resolute."

As a result, I decided to protest the Till murder at once by introducing a resolution to name a small South Side park for Emmett Till. At this time the city government still administered dozens of small parks, most of them unnamed. I chose one in Englewood, then a racially changing area where Emmett had lived, and I prepared a suitably strong resolution to name it for him.

The resolution caused an aldermanic and public uproar. Alderman John Egan told me: "You have made such a good impression in the city council and have such a fine record so far. Why do you spoil it with this resolution about Emmett Till?" I had, on Bill Townsend's advice, stuck my neck out. From then on, I never ever pulled it back in.

I was determined about that resolution, but it went to committee and never emerged. All the Daley aldermen, black and white, turned away. So did the Republicans. (More than forty years later, in 1999, when Chicago African Americans wanted to name a street for Emmett Till, every alderman voted for it.)

THE TILL resolution was a point of departure for my aldermanic career. Soon after, in 1956, came my advocacy of fair-housing legislation for Chicago. Today, it is and has long been the law of city, state, and nation, but then it was widely and vehemently opposed.

The *New York Times* had reported a fair-housing ordinance passed by the New York City Council. We needed one in Chicago. The idea of such an ordinance was then so explosive that I realized I would have to try to build support before even introducing it. Discreetly, I circulated a copy of my ordinance with a statement in favor of it. There was no material response, however, until one day the *Chicago Daily News*, an evening newspaper, carried an amazing page-one headline, "Holman and Despres Back Fair Housing Law." That was my first news of Alderman Holman's interest.

This was so much more than I expected—a black ally from the Daley ranks. I had despaired of ever finding one. Furthermore, the headline opened the explosive issue to wide public discussion. For months thereafter I gave interviews, wrote columns, and talked about a fair-housing law. Organizations I had never known or penetrated asked me to speak. When I was invited to address the Dearborn Real Estate Board—a black real estate organization—Daley supporters objected to my appearance, but its president, Dempsey Travis, stood firm, and I spoke.

Alderman Claude Holman's cosponsorship, which I welcomed with warmth and relief, had an unusual origin and, for me but not for him, a strange outcome. He used fair housing to crack Boss Dawson's power over him.

Holman was a bright, aggressive lawyer. He had organized his 1955 aldermanic victory over a tired, old, white Republican alderman in the racially changing Fourth Ward, adjoining my Fifth Ward.

In 1956, he was elected ward committeeman also. He was part of the Dawson-controlled committeemen, but he was too ambitious to continue as a subordinate. William Dawson was a congressman, but his political power came from his control of all patronage in every ward with a black committeeman. A few years earlier—before Daley— one of those committeemen, Christopher Wimbish, had quarreled with Dawson and tried to show independence. Dawson simply notified the Democratic Party headquarters to cut off all his patronage. Wimbish then ceased being effective as a committeeman because he could no longer have anyone hired or fired. He was finished as head of his ward's patronage army and found himself replaced.

In the 1955 election, Dawson had thrown the decisive support of black wards to Daley. He assured Daley's victory in the primary election fight against two adversaries, former mayor Martin Kennelly and former Chicago corporation counsel Benjamin Adamowski. With his multiward patronage, Dawson also controlled the black vote in the city council.

In my own 1955 aldermanic election, Dawson's personal allies in the Fifth Ward had supported my opponent, but my ward was considered to be white and Dawson did not send in forces to capture it. My victory could only have irked him into marking me as someone to defeat when the ward might become more black. That was just what Bill Townsend had warned me about.

Dawson was a great accommodationist. Personally, he had endured racial discrimination and could orate forcefully about it. But beyond seeking more offices and more patronage jobs for blacks in wards he controlled, he did nothing significant about racial discrimination. In exchange for keeping things quiet and turning in huge majorities, he was treated handsomely by the party Machine.

When New York City passed its fair-housing ordinance, Dawson sent word to his group that there was to be no effort to enact an ordinance in Chicago. Such a drive would have cracked Dawson's basic arrangement with the mayor, and the mayor's policy was against fair housing. Daley wanted to protect white areas from black incursion so far as he possibly could. As for Dawson, he simply awaited the steadily expanding ghetto, which slowly gave him more wards he expected to control. So the word for the black aldermen was "No fair-housing activity."

Holman saw that his joining my fair-housing campaign would be a way to signal his freedom from Dawson and also to make himself appear as a citywide champion of civil rights. Consequently, he leaked his fair-housing support to *Chicago Daily News* reporter Jay

McMullen, and the dramatic headline ensued. I was naive. I thought Holman was supporting fair housing because he believed in it. No other alderman was publicly for it.

Holman's war of independence with Dawson went on for a year or more. While it lasted, Holman cooperated fully with me on local aldermanic matters. He cosigned ordinances for parking meters and traffic regulation on streets that went through both of our wards, but I could never get him to agree to introduce the fair-housing ordinance.

"This is not the time," he would say. He meant that he was negotiating and wanted to keep his options open.

At first I was satisfied to wait. The campaign to build public opinion was proceeding well. I knew that a hostile mayor and city council could kill the ordinance outright. For a while, I too believed that "this was not the time." Finally, I decided that this was the time, but I could not get Holman to budge. Once, when a long seasonal recess was about to occur, he told me, "Next meeting," but when the next meeting came, it was still "not the time." While Holman was using fair housing to defy Dawson, he was withholding action as a way to reassure Daley that there was nothing to fear.

Eventually, my fair-housing romance with Holman came to an end. One morning I arrived for a city council meeting and found Holman circulating a resolution. It was an innocuous unenforceable document about housing on which he had already obtained signatures of twenty-five or thirty Daley aldermen. I saw at once that he and the Daley administration had united, and he was giving up on fair housing.

"Why are you doing this?" I asked. "What we need to do is introduce our ordinance."

He answered curtly, "I think this is the best way to proceed."

From then on I was on my own for fair housing. No one else supported it. Also, Holman stopped cooperating on the smallest issues.

Holman's sell-out told everyone he had made a deal, and the scope of it soon became apparent. Daley had stepped in as an apparent peacemaker between Holman and Dawson and had frozen patronage in the Fourth Ward. During the freeze, neither Holman nor Dawson could vise, that is, discharge, any of the 250 or 350 patronage appointees who made up Holman's political army. Far from being an impartial move by Daley, the freeze destroyed Dawson's power to vise Holman's troops, a power that would have enabled Dawson to topple Holman as he had destroyed Wimbish.

The freeze shifted Holman's source of power from Dawson to Daley, and in short order every other black committeeman was also put in direct line to Daley. Congressman Dawson was reduced to committeeman of only his own Second Ward. There was no public disgrace, just a surgical removal of multiward power from Dawson to Daley.

For years, the general uninformed public continued to view Dawson as political boss of blacks, but he was a shorn ram. Daley was in command and was free to designate his own new black committeeman whenever a white candidate became unelectable in a racially changed ward.

After that, Holman grew vitriolic in his attacks against me and superlaudatory in his praise of the mayor. Daley loved such praise—no matter how idiotic—and impassively savored every word. One day in the city council, Holman shouted, "In my book, you are the greatest mayor Chicago has ever had. You are the greatest mayor in the world, and in outer space too."

Holman never surpassed that praise, nor did he ever again do anything independent to advance civil rights or end discrimination.

Despite Holman's apostasy, his earlier support of fair housing had been invaluable. It gave a biracial tone to my advocacy. The idea of fair housing had been advanced. In the city council, I was certainly established as an enemy of racial discrimination.

When there was a debate about racial discrimination, the administration adopted the system of designating black aldermen to answer me. On other issues, it designated Jewish aldermen, unless Alderman Keane felt he was the only one who could reply adequately. As a result, Aldermen Paul Wigoda, Mayer Goldberg, Bert Natarus, and other Jewish aldermen would jump up on general issues and rebut me. On racial issues Claude Holman, Kenneth Campbell, William Harvey, and other dependable black aldermen were constrained to speak against their deepest personal interests.

The public effect of the Daley black aldermen ganging up on me was the opposite of what the administration planned. After television entered the city council chambers in 1960, viewers saw six Daley black aldermen jumping on someone who was fighting to end racial discrimination. They became known as the Silent Six because they did not speak out against racial discrimination. In 1968 the *Negro Digest* called me the "lone 'Negro' spokesman in Chicago's city council." The supreme accolade came one day in city council when Holman called me a "n—— lover."

At times, non-Jewish white aldermen were also pressed into service. From time to time, Alderman Krska would rise and shout briefly, "Alderman Despres is never satisfied. I say, 'God bless Mayor Daley.'" He would always get great applause.

As floor leader, Alderman Tom Keane reserved the right, if he thought only he could clarify, of giving the final answer to me on city business but never on racial segregation.

Once Alderman Paul Wigoda, white and Jewish, took it on himself to answer me as to housing discrimination. "Alderman Despres says Chicago is residentially the most segregated big city," he said. "That is not true. The Urban League has shown that Cleveland is more segregated." Some answer!

An Endless Fight for Equality

14

He [Despres] represented the Black community even though he wasn't Black and represented the poor even though he wasn't poor.

Alderman Dick Simpson, *Hyde Park Herald*, April 16, 1975

MY SECOND election increased my self-confidence in the city council decisively. The experience I had with Hyde Park urban renewal encouraged me to continue to press strongly for city planning, but my most effective efforts were clearly for measures to correct racial injustices. My council chamber sallies on comprehensive planning were treated with disdain. Daley simply wanted to be free of planning restrictions.

Raising racial issues was quite different. There was always immediate tension among the Daley black aldermen because they knew they should be on the same side but had to get up to denounce me as a faker. There was tension too among white aldermen who knew the racial issue was crucial.

In 1959, I became relentless in opposing racial discrimination in housing, schools, and public employment and facilities. I was alone on the issue from 1959 to 1963, among forty-seven Daley aldermen and two Republicans who were not interested in fighting racial segregation.

After 1963, invaluable allies arrived in the city council—Aldermen William Cousins Jr. and A. A. "Sammy" Rayner. Daley remained unregenerate. He fought equality all the way. Even in 1975, he was easily reelected and would have been elected again in 1979 if he had lived. But by 1971, he was beginning to lose full control of his party.

Daley had warnings in 1972, when he lost the Illinois delegation to the Democratic Convention, and again in 1974 in the congressional primary election, when he tried to crush rebellious Congressman Ralph Metcalfe by putting up a heavy, blue-ribbon candidate, Erwin France, Ph.D. Instead, France was crushed by 85 percent of the vote.

Thanks partly to television exposure that began in 1960, each city council attack on me brought more public support, especially from blacks. The opportunities for effectively raising this key issue were immense, because the discriminatory pattern was so pervasive. I introduced ordinances and resolutions, opposed appointments, proposed amendments, questioned appointees and witnesses, developed budget proposals, demanded information, and moved to bring buried measures out of committee. The Daley administration always had all the votes it needed to enforce its will, but it could not bury an issue.

The city council rules were skewed to make as many motions as possible undebatable. The Daley administration would have liked to suppress all unfavorable debate, but public disapproval of such repression would have been too great. The press, including television after 1960, was always present to report it.

The rules limited an alderman's remarks to ten minutes, but I never talked even that long more than once or twice in twenty years. One reason was that ten minutes exceeded the general attention span, but the compelling reason was that I would lose the microphone and the floor long before the ten-minute limit. When I began to say something that might be an effective press item, the floor leader or the mayor arranged to have an administration alderman call "Point of order," which requires immediate recognition.

"State your point of order, Alderman," the mayor would say, and my microphone was turned off and the challenger's was switched on by an electrician following the mayor's order.

The alderman would invent some point of order about what I was saying, and the mayor would respond, "Your point of order is well taken," and then recognize some other alderman to speak.

At first, I objected to being deprived of the floor, but I soon understood that protest was futile. I had to say what I wanted to say in a minute or two, before being cut off. This was good training in public speaking for the rest of my life.

On my last day in the council, when a few aldermen rose to make speeches about my departure, Alderman Terence Gabinski, Congressman Dan Rostenkowski's man, said, "When Alderman Despres got up to talk, if the resolution was about Howdy Doody, before you knew it he was talking about racial segregation."

Often the replies by the black aldermen—especially Alderman Holman—were savage attacks on me, with variations on the basic theme that I was insincere. Eventually, a new routine developed. Some appointment or ordinance would be brought up that the administration hoped to pass unanimously without comment. I was prepared and would rise and state a strong point before being cut off. Because the administration believed it could not allow my position to stand unanswered, one black alderman after another would rise to answer.

Occasionally, even a white Daley stalwart would have something to say. One such alderman had a mantra: "If Jesus Christ were appointed to office, Alderman Despres would object." The final vote would be forty-nine to one or forty-seven to three, and I would be dealt another "crushing defeat."

Only it wasn't a defeat. In my 1959 campaign, I had learned to let personal abuse roll off my back like raindrops off a duck. I used to think, These guys believe they are winning a great victory. They are only weakening their position, infuriating their constituents, and fortifying the general movement against racial segregation.

Outside the city council I was also active. I spoke whenever asked, on radio and television. I often took part in peaceful demonstrations, parades, or picketing.

After the 1963 election, when I was no longer alone in the city council, Aldermen William Cousins, Sammy Rayner, and I became staunch colleagues. Charles Chew and Fred Hubbard, for whom I campaigned, also entered the city council, but both of them became Daley supporters. Bill Cousins was splendid and strong in every way. Sammy Rayner was dependable but lacked eloquence. I felt much less lonely. Their presence was a sign of the times. Nationally, the Congress was liberalizing laws. In Chicago, sentiment against racial segregation was strengthening.

It would take eight years, though, for my critical efforts for fair housing to ripen into an ordinance. Finally, after the federal government enacted civil rights laws, Daley could no longer blatantly resist the tide. The Daley black aldermen, I am sure, told him he was jeopardizing their electability by forcing them to defend a segregationist policy in full television view of their constituents.

Daley's challenge was to pass a fair-housing ordinance that would appear to some as a good step but would accomplish, as much as possible, nothing. The fair-housing plan Daley prepared was close to being a segregationist's ideal. It created a commission with a procedure for investigation and enforcement so prolonged and drawn out that its power to make any change was almost zero. Nevertheless, this symbol of fair housing was so abhorrent to racists in a few white neighborhoods that three or four Daley aldermen said in self-defense that they could not vote for it.

It was sent to the Judiciary Committee, of which I was a member. No public hearing was held. Members were notified of a meeting, but it was not held in one of the usual committee rooms on the second or third floors of City Hall but rather in a conference room of the Law Department on the fifth floor. This was the only time in twenty years that a committee of which I was a member met there. Unfortunately, I arrived five minutes late at the Law Department reception desk. Obviously under orders, the receptionist refused to let me enter. No excuse. I was just barred. After about ten minutes, I was admitted. The ordinance had been recommended.

The mayor had attended the meeting by using a direct passageway from his own fifth-floor office. I can only imagine what he said to the committee because no one ever told me. His position was: "This is a measure we have to pass for the sake of the party. It is reasonable. It has many safeguards built into it. It provides for a thorough, fair, and *long* investigation by staff before anything can go forward. There are several levels of review before the commission can enter an order. The commission will be appointed by me, and I will choose persons whom the city can count on for fairness. Then the provisions call for full review by the courts. This is an ordinance that no Chicagoan needs to fear. I am sure you aldermen know that under present conditions this action must be taken."

On the city council floor, Paul Corcoran was one of the aldermen who voted against the ordinance. He represented the then-white Austin community on the Far West Side, which was fearing a black flood from the overcrowded adjacent communities. He said privately he would be politically dead if he ever voted to pass an ordinance that favored even the principle of fair housing. He voted against it. Nothing happened to Corcoran immediately, but this is what he told me a couple of years later:

"I had an important appointment awaiting action in the mayor's office. It was politically very important to me. Month after month went by, and no word. I called the mayor's office for an appointment, and they said they would call back. No call. I called again. Still no return. Finally after several calls and about a year after the fair-housing vote, they called me to set an appointment, and I went to see the mayor. Before I said anything, the mayor swung his desk chair around to face me and said, 'Paul, you hurt me.' Then he scolded me for about fifteen minutes without stopping. That was the end of the interview. Nothing was said about the appointment. About two months later it came through."

Alderman James Murray from a white Southwest Side ward also had a constituency hostile to fair housing. During all his years in the city council he had supported Daley on every relevant roll call. He knew he would be politically dead if he voted for the ordinance, however benign it seemed. Daley promised to take care of him, and he voted aye. In the next election he was defeated over his fair-housing vote. The party rewarded him with election as a judge.

In practice, the fair-housing ordinance created what Daley wanted—a weak, passive, ineffective agency, without initiative. Like Aesop's sparrow on the flying eagle's back, it never attained status until federal law enforcement lifted it high enough. I peppered the city agency with requests for action. Repeatedly I sent them for-rent ads from buildings that kept out nonwhites. Its director, Ed Marciniak, always had excuses. I think every stimulating barb I sent him must have made him uncomfortable. Years and years later, he took his revenge of sorts. I spoke about Chicago politics at an American Historical Association meeting and compared the tactics of Edward Vrdolyak, who made political use of gangs and money, with those of the early Hitler. Afterward Marciniak came up, warmly congratulated me, and asked for a copy of my talk. He then gave it to a racial ethics committee and charged me with racist linking of a local politico to Hitler. The charge was not sustained.

My course was set. I was personally friendly with Daley, but I could not back off on racial segregation. On the contrary, I felt the need to show my constituents that his support of me in my 1963 election had not bought silence on this issue.

In March of that year, at the first meeting after my third election, I made a special point of speaking out on a resolution about racial discrimination in the fire department. Discrimination there was shameful, worse than in the police department.

One of Police Superintendent Orlando W. Wilson's first actions in 1960 had been to put racially mixed pairs of officers in patrol cars. In the fire department, the city yielded to vociferous, bigoted firefighters who did not want blacks to share their sleeping quarters at fire stations.

Because firefighters and police officers and their families represented more than fifty thousand votes, Daley yielded to racial prejudices in their ranks and resisted measures to end departmental bias.

The inflow of African Americans to those departments was resisted in every way possible—by rigid physical examinations, by oral examinations, by production of arrest records, and finally by prolonged legal resistance to the federal government's lawsuits to lift discrimination. The mayor hired Richard Phelan, a tough white trial lawyer, and Earl Neal, a polished African American lawyer, to defend the suits with all possible energy.

Although inevitably some black applicants found their way through Daley's maze into the fire department, they were kept in segregated firehouses with sleeping quarters for blacks only. In 1963 in all Chicago I could find only one African American firefighter in a white fire station, at Forty-sixth and Cottage Grove, at the edge of the black ghetto.

In March 1963, when I attacked fire department segregation, I hit a live nerve, and after the city council meeting Daley complained to Fifth Ward committeeman Marshall Korshak about me. I do not know what Korshak said to Daley to bolster his own position, but there was nothing he could do about me, and that is what he probably told Daley: "I can't do anything about Despres either."

In 1968, I had an ardent but brief leap of hope when Martin Luther King Jr. came to Chicago. His arrival attracted to his side significant numbers of supporting clergy and dedicated laypeople. Daley's attitude was "King, who needs him?" but I thought I saw the local movement I had been waiting for. Although not part of Dr. King's project, I was invited to give an address on Chicago politics to his Saturday-morning meeting. I thought it would give me an opportunity to help them toward political victory.

Their headquarters in a West Side church was filled with 150 to 200 King workers, but King was not present. I talked for thirty to forty minutes and received rapt attention. I discussed the Chicago political patronage system and fully outlined the Machine's political domination. I explained how to acquire political influence, the need to organize in the precincts, and how to elect candidates committed to ending segregation. Political organization, I told them, was the only thing Daley feared. The applause was loud and strong. My whole audience, I assumed, was sympathetic.

An aide to Dr. King then stood up to demolish what I said. "If we follow Despres's advice, we would be doing just what our enemies do. We would be making ourselves just like our enemies." And on and on. That was the end. No questions, no discussion. The line had been handed down. Years later the aide became a Republican candidate in a southern state.

I still wonder if that aide were not an infiltrator. He was bad-mouthing the only steps that could lead to ending entrenched segregation in Chicago. I feared at once that with such leadership the Chicago King Project would soon go nowhere. Some of the clergymen I knew there were abashed and shamefaced at what the aide had said, but they could do nothing except go along with the prestigious project.

From then on, the project staged demonstrations week after week, but Daley's fears about Dr. King dissipated. There was no political action. The demonstrations were no threat to Daley. Far from it. The TV pictures terrified many whites, whose support of Daley became indissoluble. As a result, the mayor earned an undeserved civil rights good point by using police personnel to protect the demonstrators, and one protest after another backfired. They attracted thousands of King followers, but finally his supporters just became fatigued, and Daley, more entrenched. The walls of Chicago-Jericho did not come tumbling down.

ONE SATURDAY morning I received an emergency telephone call. A voice said, "There will be an emergency meeting this morning at eleven o'clock about Dr. King for all black public officeholders at the South Side YMCA at Fifty-first and Wabash. Please be there." I was overcome. This was the ultimate acceptance of me as a "black" officeholder. Many times, white people who saw me in person for the first time had expressed astonishment that I was white. My strong championship of the rights of blacks caused many white people to assume I was African American. But here was a summons from a sophisticated black person to a meeting of "all black public office-holders."

We "black representatives" met in a classroom of the YMCA building. I was the only white person. Soon Dr. King arrived. He was serious, low-key, and disarmingly frank. "We need a victory. We are at the end and we have to leave. But we need a victory." For me it was very sad, this end of the line and this disingenuous plea for help in obtaining a disengagement that might look like a victory.

Ralph Metcalfe, still then a Daley alderman, could hardly conceal his satisfaction. "Let us put our arms around you, Dr. King. Let us put our arms around you." And he did put an arm around Dr. King. There was a bustle, a telephone call, and Metcalfe and others said, "We'll go to City Hall. They're waiting for us."

Metcalfe, Dr. King, and several Daley supporters walked out quickly. I was not invited. I was perplexed. Apparently there was some arrangement to which I was clearly not a party.

The "victory" for Dr. King was arranged. At City Hall the Leadership Council for Metropolitan Chicago was formed and financial support was pledged. It then engaged in fighting housing segregation in the white suburbs. By the end of seven years it had succeeded in placing families in suburban dwellings, at the average rate of fourteen families per year. The director, Kale Williams, the staff, and the volunteers deserve great credit for their hard work. But one hundred families was not much of a victory for Martin Luther King Jr.

Nothing else I did as alderman approached the importance and effectiveness of my unending (and still unfinished) work against segregation. Nothing else had similar impact.

Chicago Children Die from Lead Poisoning

15

It is difficult for us to understand what small amounts of lead were capable of killing children.

Gerald Markowitz and David Rosner, *Deceit and Denial*

Those mothers should watch their babies so they don't chop holes in the walls.

Landlord of an apartment where a baby died from ingesting lead paint chips, *Chicago Daily News*, October 12, 1968

IN THE early summer of 1967, the *Chicago Sun-Times* reported that a child in the Fifth Ward had died from ingesting flakes of lead paint. It described the dwelling place in Woodlawn and explained that children play on the floor, the flakes on the floor have a sweet taste, children eat them, and soon a brain is fatally affected.

This was a danger from poor housing. It was definitely up to the city to deal with it. Only the municipality could do so. I decided I must do what I could to push for action.

On my prompt visit to the family whose child had died, I saw two other children continuing to play on the floor, picking up scraps of old paint and eating them. One would expect a humane and responsible city government to be immediately concerned. Not so.

The city had full power to regulate housing conditions. I prepared an ordinance to declare a residence with interior lead paint to be a public nuisance. Then the city or any tenant on the premises could compel the owner to abate the nuisance. I enlisted the help and cooperation of Aldermen Bill Cousins and Sammy Rayner, both of whom stayed with the ordinance to the end.

It was introduced on July 21, 1967, and on July 23, a one-year-old girl, Gwendolyn Rush, died of lead poisoning on the West Side. Also on July 23, Brian Pendleton, age two, died of lead poisoning at 6416 South Minerva Avenue. On August 11, Drusilla Gordon, aged two and a half, died on the West Side in a house off Karlov Avenue. On August 15, Edith Prater, age two, of 3655 West Ohio, died of lead poisoning. On August 24, another two-year-old, Laura Ann Bryant, of 6937 South State Street, died of lead poisoning.

Meantime, the ordinance was simply sent to committee with nothing done about it. On August 29, a month and a week after we introduced the ordinance, a letter came from Health Commissioner Dr. Samuel Andelman, saying that it would be a "monumental job" to enforce the proposed ordinance. Merely to determine the amount of lead in the paint, the letter said, would be most difficult. On September 4, Cathy Boone, age two, of 5736 South Marshfield Avenue, died of lead poisoning.

Granting that the ordinance might be hard to enforce, we introduced a resolution in September to overcome Dr. Andelman's letter. It called on the Board of Health to submit a plan "to bring an immediate end to the continued existence of lead poisonous premises." It was referred to committee. On October 1, Demetria Thompson, one year old, of 1108 South Little, died of lead poisoning.

Finally, some nine months after the ordinance was introduced, the City Council Committee on Health held a hearing on it. Only eight days later, on April 13, Sherez Johnson, age two, of 3441 West Madison Street, died of lead poisoning.

At one point during this epidemic, I was invited to a medical presentation about lead poisoning at the University of Chicago hospitals. There was a pretty two-year-old who was being chelated against lead poisoning but who had not been completely cured. Chelation is a medical procedure for removing lead from the human body. The case was explained in medical terms, but what was impressive was the dullness of the child, the obvious effect of the lead poisoning. Even complete chelation does not remove all the traces of brain damage.

The lead poisoning scene was appalling. Clearly most parents were not aware of the slow death that awaited their children in these homes. It was also clear that most of the homes where lead paint chips were being consumed were in poverty areas, particularly in segregated, black areas.

This was an emergency. We made contact with medical personnel also interested in doing something. Dr. Quentin Young responded at once and formed the Chicago Committee against Lead Poisoning, headed by Dr. Agnes Latimer, a pediatrician at Michael Reese Hospital. The committee called for a strong ordinance and recruited the support of nineteen civic and community organizations and more than one hundred prominent physicians, clergymen, and other civic leaders. The committee also collected signatures on petitions.

The chairman of the City Council Committee on Health, Alderman Ralph Metcalfe, appointed a subcommittee headed by Alderman Mayer Goldberg to "study the matter further." Meantime, every few days brought another report of a child dying of lead poisoning from old paint chips. The Goldberg subcommittee met July 1, 1968, and approved a substitute ordinance against flaked paint, with no mention of lead poisoning.

In the meantime, there were four more deaths from lead paint. These children lived in substandard housing, put things in their mouths, swallowed them, and died.

On August 8, the Building and Zoning Committee met and the Goldberg substitute was given full committee approval, even though it did not mention lead poisoning. It was reported into the city council on August 13 with a committee recommendation for passage. The substitute ordinance would simply have required that interior surfaces of residential buildings be kept free of flaking, peeling, or chipped paint or plaster, conditions already generally prohibited by the building code under which all the listed deaths had occurred.

No action was taken by the city council, as the proposal was "published and deferred." That meant that it went to the next city council meeting.

On August 27, sixteen-month-old Dwight Simmons became the fifteenth child to die of lead poisoning since we introduced legislation to fight the problem.

On September 9, the Chicago Committee against Lead Poisoning held a press conference to denounce the watered-down Goldberg amendment and to call for a strong ordinance to strengthen the city's hand. If it passed, landlords would be made financially liable for causing lead poisoning. We believed that the financial-liability provision would guarantee a good measure of enforcement, which was particularly important in light of the city administration's indifference.

On September 11, the Goldberg substitute was due for a vote, but the administration did not call it up or even mention it. Between then and October 8, the city administration began retreating slightly. It abandoned the Goldberg measure as no longer expedient. In the mayor's office, Deputy Mayor David Stahl played a central role. He met with Dr. Eric Oldberg, president of the board of health; others from the city administration; Dr. Agnes Latimer from the Metropolitan Housing and Planning Council and the Chicago Committee against Lead Poisoning; and George Ranney Jr. from the Metropolitan Housing and Planning Council. They were shown a draft of a compromise ordinance.

On October 9, Alderman Metcalfe presented as his own a new administration lead-poisoning ordinance. The full council adopted it thirty-nine to one. It seemed not nearly strong enough. Unlike the Goldberg proposal, however, it made specific reference to lead as a potential "hazard to the health and safety to the occupants of the family unit."

The Metcalfe ordinance outlawed paint and plaster containing more than 1 percent lead or its compounds. It did not declare such buildings to be public nuisances, but it empowered the building commissioner to obtain samples and conduct analyses, something that Health Commissioner Andelman had said the city could not do.

On the day of passage, speaking separately but in almost identical language, Alderman Metcalfe and Dr. Oldberg both told the press that it "was not the Despres ordinance that was passed."

Council Colleagues Go to Prison 16

I let them go so far and no farther.

Mayor Richard J. Daley to University of Chicago professors
at the Quadrangle Club

CHICAGO ALDERMEN represent their wards and share a duty to help
govern the city. While many have done so to the best of their ability,
others have historically looked on the aldermanic office as a protected
opportunity to make money.

My Fifth Ward predecessor, Alderman Robert E. Merriam, who
later ran for mayor against Richard J. Daley in 1955, dramatized the
corruption issue by exposing a city building inspector who had taken
a bribe. But Merriam found himself thwarted in trying to prove his
charges. He was himself accused of persecution and denounced for
harassing a "defenseless city employee."

An earlier chapter discussed aldermanic payoffs for driveway permits. Despite the long and open traffic, no alderman was ever indicted,
much less convicted, for driveway permit extortion. In my twenty
years in the city council, I found corruption in the city council easy to
suspect but hard to establish and impossible to get the city to act against.

On March 19, 1969, a measure came before the city council that
was designed to rezone a large tract of land at Western and Pratt.
It had formerly been a golf club. Approval of the change would
increase the land's dollar value by millions and allow exploitation for
business uses, high-rises, and multiple-housing units.

I rose to my feet and said, "There is an aura of corruption about this
ordinance. I can even say there is an aroma of corruption. Perhaps

this ordinance will pass, but it shouldn't. If it does, the mayor must veto it." That was strong language, but my feelings about it were strong. From the rostrum, Daley smiled at me indulgently. I sensed that the city council was going to pass the ordinance and that he was not going to veto it. The skids were greased.

I wondered why a mayor who was reputed not to take bribes himself would tolerate evident dishonesty by party members. As he told a group of University of Chicago professors at a closed meeting, referring to his organization allies, "I let them go so far and no farther." Perhaps this corrupt ordinance was the "so far" he meant. Murder? No. Payment for a rezoning ordinance? OK. The rezoning passed. Later, the U.S. attorney was able to establish that Alderman Paul Wigoda had received fifty thousand dollars for help on passage of the ordinance. For this, he eventually went to prison.

That financial corruption was going on around me was proved because eleven of the aldermen who served with me in the city council were later indicted, convicted, and imprisoned. For details, see the end of this chapter. Only one alderman who was indicted was acquitted. I could merely surmise how extensive corruption was and how many more than the eleven convicted also should have been sent to prison. In the golf course case, though, the stench was so pungent that I had to speak out, even though I could not then actually prove extortion or bribery.

On one other occasion, I did engage in a foray about fiscal corruption. The press charged that Alderman Keane had bought Chicago Skyway bonds on the strength of insider knowledge that the City of Chicago was planning to make up some missing interest payments. This would cause the bonds to jump in value. When I referred to the accusation on the city council floor, Keane rose to deny it and said with bravado, "My records are open for anyone to inspect." He said he welcomed anyone to do so.

I announced that I accepted his offer. What followed was a week of futile efforts and encounters with stone walls. Telephone calls, letters, demands on Keane or his brokers in Chicago or New York all went unanswered. I could get no records. After a week or ten days, I had to give up.

Recommendations of legislative action, as they came from a committee or a city department, had been washed clean of any indication of who got what long before the measures ever reached the city council floor. To prove corruption required the resources of a U.S. attorney or a Cook County state's attorney who was not affiliated with the Democratic Party of Cook County. When I had suspicions that tempted me to make accusations but no hard proof, I had to say to myself, "Remember Bob Merriam and his building inspector."

In the Chicago City Council, the opportunity for corruption was there. I saw five waves of aldermen come into public office, and I could almost hear some new aldermen say to themselves, "This is my chance."

Useful efforts against corruption occasionally came from investigative expeditions by the *Chicago Tribune*, the *Chicago Sun-Times*, the Better Government Association, and most effectively by the U.S. Department of Justice. With one exception, the Cook County state's attorney, on the other hand, has established a record of tolerating general corruption. A single exception that showed how effective the state's attorney could be when he is independent of the Machine was Republican Benjamin Adamowski, who held the position from 1956 to 1960. In a single term, he managed to uncover and end, at least temporarily, several wholesale patterns of city corruption.

The political Machine is careful to insulate aldermen from the investigative tools necessary to prove corruption. For example, Richard J. Daley had the city council pass an ordinance creating a Department of Investigation. This sounded fine, but the commissioner of investigation was responsible only to the mayor and was bound by law not to disclose anything to anyone else. There is no record of his ever disclosing anything to anyone.

For self-protection, the Machine exerts strong efforts to elect friendly state's attorneys, as much as mayors.

Convicted Colleagues

1. Thomas Keane (Thirty-first), was floor leader of the city council for Mayor Daley from 1958 until his conviction for mail fraud and conspiracy in 1974. He used his influence and inside knowledge to buy 218 parcels of tax-delinquent property and then sell them at a profit to government agencies. At his trial, I testified that when I voted to approve the sales, I had no information that they were fraudulent or that he was the real buyer. Keane was in the city council in 1955 when Benjamin B. Becker had to be dropped as the city clerk candidate from Daley's first ticket for mayor because Becker voted to pass ordinances in which he had a direct secret financial interest. In the city council, Keane—once my ally in passing the ordinance that ended aldermanic extortion for driveway permits—had never let up in his praise of Daley. Keane served twenty-two months in prison.

2. Paul Wigoda (Forty-ninth), a longtime member of the city council, shared law offices with Alderman Keane and was considered his protégé. He was convicted in 1974 for accepting $50,000 for supporting a zoning change that involved the former Edgewater Golf Club. The property was in an adjacent ward. It was zoned as residential, and he had it rezoned for high-rises and business uses, thus increasing its value by millions of dollars. Wigoda was sentenced to a year and a day in prison and subsequently was reinstated as a lawyer.

3. Fred Roti was the alderman of the First Ward, sometimes referred to as "the syndicate ward." Because he sat in the first chair on the floor of the city council, he was the first to vote on any matter. In contested matters, he would get a signal from the floor leader and, by his oral vote, communicate it to the other organization aldermen. He was convicted of taking a $10,000 bribe for influencing a civil court case and $7,500 for support of a zoning change. He was caught because the government had placed a hidden microphone in the Counselors' Row restaurant, across from City Hall on LaSalle Street, where he ate lunch daily. He was sentenced to three and a half years in prison.

4. Tyrone Kenner (Third), a former Chicago police officer, was a promising black political leader but a part of the Machine. In

1983, he was convicted of taking $15,500 in bribes to help more than a dozen people get Cook County sheriff's deputy jobs and to enable two persons to receive passing grades on the examination for city electrician. He was sentenced to twenty months in prison. Later, he ran for alderman twice in an effort to return to the city council, but he lost both times.

Machine Democrats were not the only aldermen caught. The Republicans also had their convicts, as noted in some of the following listings.

5. Casimir Staszcuk (Thirteenth) was a Republican. On occasion, he would vote against a Daley proposal, but only rarely. He was convicted in 1973 of accepting bribes for zoning amendments and was sentenced to a year and a half in prison.

6. Edward Scholl (Forty-first) had a solid base on the Northwest Side and was elected on an anti-Daley Republican platform, but he often voted to support the mayor's measures. He pleaded guilty to accepting $7,800 in bribes for zoning changes. He was sentenced to eighteen months.

7. Joseph Potempa (Twenty-third), another Republican, blended into the background in the city council. He was convicted for accepting $3,000 in bribes and of not reporting $9,000 in bribes as income. He was sentenced to a year and a day in prison.

8. Frank Kuta (Twenty-third), a Machine Democrat, succeeded Joseph Potempa as alderman of his West Side ward. It took him approximately a year to be caught for taking a bribe that was half the amount his predecessor was caught taking. He received six months, only half the sentence Potempa had received.

9. Wallace Davis Jr. (Twenty-seventh) a West Side alderman and a 100 percent Machine Democrat, was convicted in 1987 for receiving a $5,000 bribe from an FBI informant and $11,000 in kickbacks from his ward secretary, who was his niece. He was sentenced to three years in prison.

10. Fred Hubbard (Second) seemed to be a promising liberal Democrat, but he was convicted in 1972 for embezzling nearly $100,000 from a federally funded jobs program. He was sentenced to two years in prison.

11. Stanley Zydlo (Twenty-sixth), yet another nominal Republican, was not sentenced for accepting bribes but for paying one. He gave $1,000 to alter the fire department test scores for two relatives. He was sentenced to six months in a prison-release program.

12. Lawrence Bloom (Fifth), who succeeded me as alderman from Hyde Park, received my support when he ran for that office and also in his campaign for state's attorney. In December 1998, he pleaded guilty to income tax evasion. In the plea agreement, he admitted accepting $14,000 from an FBI mole for approving a dump-site permit. He also admitted to deflecting constituents' complaints against it. He had allowed the rock-crushing work to continue in return for the bribe. He was sentenced to six months in the federal minimum-security prison in Wisconsin. Until news of the bribes, I had considered him a good alderman.

Here are some other convictions:

Alderman	Ward	Offense	Year	Sentence
13. Donald Swinarski	12	$7,800 zoning bribe	1975	4 months
14. William Corruthers	28	Having Bethany Hospital do work for his ward office	1983	3 years
15. Jesse Evans	21	Bribes and $10,000 in extortion money	1997	41 months
16. John Madrzyk	13	Ghost payrolling and kickbacks	1998	41 months
17. Louis Farina	36	$7,000 bribes for city building permits	1983	1 year
18. Clifford Kelly	20	$6,500 bribe from Waste Management	1987	9 months
19. Perry Hutchinson	9	$42,200 from an FBI mole and insurance fraud	1988	11 years
20. Marion Humes	8	$5,000 from Hutchinson and $5,000 from FBI mole	1989	6 months of work release (worsening diabetic condition)
21. Allan Streeter	17	$37,000 from FBI mole	1996	8 months

Daley's Police Spy on Me

17

Daley's gumshoes spied on [Despres] for years. . . .
He was even tailed to a Halloween benefit party in 1972
at the First Unitarian Church on 57th Street.

M. W. Newman, in *Congressional Record*, February 2, 1995

WITHOUT my knowledge, the Daley administration at city expense continuously shadowed my political activity throughout my twenty years as alderman. I learned about it in my nineteenth year in office after a group of lawyers, including Matthew Piers, filed suits in 1974 entitled *Alliance to End Repression and American Civil Liberties Union v. City of Chicago.*

Under the right to deposition, they obtained detailed access to approximately five hundred thousand pages of undeleted pre-1976 files and index systems of the Chicago Police Department Intelligence Division Subversive Unit. They subsequently analyzed tens of thousands of the documents. My aldermanic activities were open and public. I had no desire to conceal them. I expected them to be carefully observed by the Fifth Ward Democratic Organization, which was always hoping to reclaim the office of alderman.

I was indignant to learn that the mayor had engaged the Chicago Police Department at public expense to observe furtively, list, and report what I was doing. After I became aware of the shadowing, I also learned that there was an individual on his staff to whom the police reports had been given.

The mayor and the Fifth Ward Democratic Organization wanted to learn what I was doing so that they could take countermeasures. They felt they needed to know and prepare. They hoped to find some compromising action on my part to bedevil me or render me politically impotent. They just wanted to know everything I was up to.

The antispying suit was filed for a number of plaintiffs (including independent alderman Dick Simpson and me), but there was no evidence of police shadowing any Machine alderman. The U.S. court held that this was a highly illegal activity in violation of the First Amendment, enjoined the City of Chicago, and awarded damages. I received ten thousand dollars.

Here are a handful of typical reports about my activities:

Will protest the use of the shoreline sites by the U.S. army to build military installations; Sun-T 3/2/56.

Will introduce a resolution in the City Council that they move to end discrimination against Negro physicians in Chicago hospitals; Sun-T 2/21/57. Member of Law and Order Committee: Chicago Commission on Human Relations: 1956.

Spoke against segregation and discrimination at mass meeting at the Chicago League of Negro Voters, July 5, 1959 at Washington Park, Chicago.

Picket Demonstration and Leaflet Demonstration City Hall, 10 July 1961, Auspices Citizens Emergency Committee for Equal Justice. Subject introduced a motion to the City Council, wherein constitutional guarantees of equal protection under the law be afforded and enforced for all citizens of Chicago, regardless of color, creed or nationality.

Subject was recognized seated in the audience at a Mass Meeting for contributions to support the Voter Registration in the South, held on 1 May 1963, at the Tabernacle Baptist Church 4130 S. Indiana Ave.

The SUBJECT seemed to be well acquainted with all of Chicago area Women for Peace pickets at the Museum of Science and Industry on 13 March 1966. He stayed and talked with the pickets for a half hour and then left at 13:45 hrs. Pickets passed out a leaflet entitled 'U.S. ACTION IN VIETNAM WAR IS NOT PEACE.' One of these pickets was the well-known Communist Eva Straus Friedlander.

INTV. RPT. SUBJECT spoke at meeting sponsored by the MEDICAL COMMITTEE FOR HUMAN RIGHTS on 4 November 1970, at 125 East 26th Street. Discussion was general.

INTV. RPT. SUBJECT attended the HYDE PARK PEACE COUNCIL rally and peace picnic at the Promontory Point, 55th Street and the Lake on 4 July 1970.

I am still angry. The city administration could not even come up with the excuse that it was fighting terrorism. Even so, it was improperly engaging in spying, misusing public funds, and building a secret record that it intended to employ as might appear useful at some time. And we taxpayers were footing the bill.

Seeking Equal Treatment for Women 18

*The history of mankind is the history of repeated injuries
and usurpations on the part of man toward woman.*

Seneca Falls Declaration of Women's Rights, July 10, 1848

THE ROLE of women today in Chicago and in city government is completely different from what it was in the 1950s, 1960s, and 1970s. A 1972 paper read at the American Political Science Association convention about women in the Daley organization reported, "The Daley women are like children as far as influence in the Cook County Democratic Party—they are to be seen and not heard."

In 1968, the city council did not have a woman alderman. Moreover, it never had had one throughout its history. Women served in the U.S. Senate, as governors, in the House of Representatives, and in the state legislatures, but not in Chicago's council chambers.

In 1972, the municipality employed women in janitorial, clerical, and stenographic positions, but very few at any level of significant responsibility. Women headed only the Alcoholic Treatment Center, the Municipal Reference Library, and the Consumer Sales Department, about 6 percent of Chicago's forty-one departments. Their total staff was only 134, or less than 0.4 percent of the city's 35,000 employees.

Chicago had no active female firefighters. There were police matrons to care for female prisoners and one lieutenant who accompanied the police commissioner at budget hearings.

During my early days in the council, this had not become as clear to me as racial discrimination had. My full awareness of how unbalanced and unfair it was did not begin until I visited the Municipal Council of Paris in late 1968. There I had the opportunity to chat with *conseillers municipaux* (aldermen) in the drinks bar adjoining the council chambers. (Libations were apparently considered a good device to enliven a city council.) Seven Parisian council members, I learned, were women. One had even given birth during her term in office. As individuals, these *Parisiennes* were making distinct contributions.

Why not in Chicago? The question needed to be pursued.

In Chicago, the absence of women aldermen was almost cast in stone. When the present City Hall was built in 1908, only one washroom was attached to the council chambers, and it was for men only. It was as if the architect and the city fathers had ordained that there should never be women in the city council. In 1966, after a fire in City Hall, the chamber was lavishly rebuilt. Again only one washroom, and it was, of course, for men. There was no awakening to the changing times.

In December 1968, I introduced a resolution to stimulate thought about women running for alderman. If it passed, the city government would call on political and nonpartisan groups to find female candidates "to break the barrier against women" in Chicago's city council.

My proposal was received with hostility and ridicule. When the press asked my adjoining Fourth Ward colleague, Alderman Holman, what he thought about it, he said: "Sex has nothing to do with it. If he feels so strongly about having a woman elected to the council, this is an excellent opportunity for him to resign so his community can elect a black woman."

Mayor Daley, given a chance to comment, responded, "Let's not discuss sex at Christmastime."

Though the resolution was steered to a committee graveyard, I was determined to keep up the fight the way I knew how: by hammering away at it with all the persistence I could summon. I was certainly aided by the improved atmosphere in the city and the country, brought on by the rise in the feminist movement. Soon, thanks to a complaint by a constituent made during aldermanic office hours, I was able to continue the fight dramatically. I learned that in city pensions, if a widowed male police officer remarried, he continued to receive his pension, but if a widow of a police officer remarried, she would lose hers. I brought this up in the form of a resolution in the city council and again drew effective publicity to the woman's issue.

Thanks to the change in the general atmosphere, the movement to end gender discrimination continued to gather strength. Although the Democratic Party of Cook County welcomed women's votes and offered female candidates for a few offices, such as the county board, it remained a male-controlled organization. Like the city council, the fifty-man army of Chicago ward committeemen, which ran the party, won the elections, and handled the patronage, was a male bastion. There had been one brief exception. Lillian Piotrowski, from the Twenty-second Ward, was briefly a committeewoman.

Finally, in 1970, a direct amendment I prepared for the city code to prohibit gender discrimination was signed by eight aldermen, from the Fifth, Sixth, Seventh, Eighth, Fortieth, Forty-third, Forty-fourth, and Forty-eighth wards. This was the first time other aldermen had joined me in the movement to crack political barriers facing women. At the time, the city government was even fighting a federal suit to cease gender discrimination in the police department.

In 1971, the campaign to change the situation in Chicago won a decidedly great victory. Two women were elected to the city council: Anna Langford, who was black, and Mary Lou Hedlund, who was white. The tradition was broken. It had taken only 134 years. As of this writing, the fifty-member city council now includes fifteen women.

The discrimination against women in the police department was then legally corrected by the judgment obtained in the federal government's suit, over city resistance. There are now women doing regular police work. The same is true in the fire department. Gender discrimination in fact has not wholly disappeared, but the resistance to it is greatly weakened.

Some female aldermen, or alderwomen, have behaved as traditionally male aldermen. The two who were elected in 1971 did not raise any particularly significant measures to deal with gender discrimination. One later alderwoman, Marion Humes, has already been listed in chapter 16 as having been convicted for extortion.

Only eleven years after my disdained resolution to recruit women to run for municipal office, Jane Byrne was elected mayor of Chicago.

My Secret Weapon

19

It's just a matter of pursuing things, really demanding services from the City, and they respond.

Despres's aldermanic office manager Annette Strickland, *Hyde Park Herald*, April 16, 1975

No one in the Machine seemed to understand the strength I was building by my rapport with constituents and my constant attention to their complaints.

Immediately after my first election, my staff (two persons) and I developed an unending effort to serve as ombudsmen for the people of the ward. It would become a secret resource, one that bonded constituents with me. They needed, I believe, to feel that they were not being ignored and that, regardless of whether or how they voted, city government would be responsive to them. Chicagoans traditionally rely on an alderman for many contacts with city government. Many Chicagoans did not (and still do not) want to make direct requests or complaints to city departments, mainly out of concern about reprisals.

My job was both to present their problems and to protect them from personal disclosure. Many Machine ward organizations used complaints or requests as devices to force citizens to "vote right" or to make citizens feel uncomfortable for having "voted wrong." Norman Elkin, my predecessor's assistant, gave me confidence when he told me, "A city department cannot ignore a letter from an alderman."

Merriam had instituted regular aldermanic office hours. I followed his practice and was available for anyone to see. We opened early on a designated evening or two and on Saturday mornings, and we stayed until the last person was taken care of. One aldermanic office was situated in Hyde Park and another in Woodlawn. As the ward boundaries shifted in the course of redistricting, additional office hours were held in South Shore.

The city allowed thirteen thousand dollars for one aldermanic assistant, and a citizens' committee raised enough for a second. It was my good fortune to have a series of excellent assistants who were on the job all day. Among them were Norah Erickson, Marshall Patner, Kenneth Gillis, and Sybil Atwood. I remember all of them with gratitude.

The city allowance for the aldermanic office expense was so meager that we had to rely on a Fifth Ward citizens' committee, originally constituted by Robert Merriam, to raise supplementary funds. The committee raised the money, and I never saw the lists of contributors.

We enjoyed massive help from volunteers. They assisted with office work, received constituents during office hours, and handled a log of requests. The office acquired an answering machine that was permanently available to receive messages and complaints from constituents at all hours. Never did we accept or hint at money in return for favors. Some Machine precinct captains who became adept at fulfilling their voters' needs did take money for doing so.

We had a simple fiscal standard laid down by Paul H. Douglas, then a U.S. senator, expressed in his short book on ethics in government. He said he had made it a rule not to accept any kind of favor or meal costing more than two dollars and fifty cents. I was grateful to him for establishing the standard but increased it to five dollars for lunch and, by the end of twenty years of modest inflation, to ten dollars.

On occasion a constituent came in and requested something like a zoning amendment, saying, "Alderman, you know you'll be taken care of." The answer always was, "No, that is not necessary. If this is in the public interest, we will work hard for it. If not, we won't."

We profited greatly from Norman Elkin's earlier advice. In every complaint that was not a pressing emergency, we not only made our own record but also sent a letter to the city agency or officer in charge. A copy went to the constituent. In this way, the constituent knew we were on the job, and the public employee or official had a written record.

The public employees were aware that if, for example, anything dire happened due to failure to respond, the record would pin responsibility. This procedure proved enormously effective, partly out of their fear of being held responsible and partly out of their pride in their work. During the 20 years, or 1,040 weeks, I was in office, we wrote more than 20 complaint letters a week, or more than 20,000 total. Every complaint was presumed important. Whatever it was, we tried to follow through promptly and in writing. The carbon copies of nearly all those letters are now part of the Despres Papers at the Chicago Historical Society.

What were those complaints? They were about abandoned cars disfiguring the neighborhood, dead alewives on the beach, buildings that needed to be demolished, potholes that could damage tires and car frames, needs for more fish in the park lagoons or more trees in barren areas, housing-code violations that caused unsafe living conditions, traffic regulations, parking shortages, streetlights, stop signs, one-way streets, and, always, racial discrimination. Each one was treated as urgent.

Using the prestige of the aldermanic office, we could apply to other agencies of government. We wrote, for example, to the proper state agency to stock fish in the Jackson Park lagoons. One weekend when a constituent had to fly to Europe immediately for his father's funeral, we phoned the passport office to get him an emergency passport.

Sometimes the answer to the constituent was that there was no prompt solution. Often we could at least obtain information. For example, we might be able to report that tree plantings would occur in such a month, or that the pothole-repair program was scheduled for April, or other information that put the constituent at ease.

From the individual complaints, we could also develop relevant general programs. When we learned, for instance, how extensive the problem of abandoned cars was, we worked to develop a program to improve the handling of abandoned cars. The ombudsman system regularly did more than just satisfy individual constituents; it expanded our knowledge of ward problems and stimulated measures to solve them.

Our office also developed a telephone guide, which we distributed widely. It listed city and other governmental agencies to call. There were still many constituents who hesitated to make a complaint directly, but we wanted to encourage them to do so when they could.

I wrote a weekly column for the *Hyde Park Herald* and also for the Woodlawn paper when there was one. Occasionally we mailed an aldermanic letter.

Through this ombudsman activity I developed a long-lasting acquaintanceship with people of the ward. It apparently was a revelation to many constituents that an alderman would do all this without fanfare, pressure, or money. It was a distinct contrast to the Machine's methods.

A myth that was particularly irritating to us was that because the alderman was not a Machine alderman, city services were not available. "I was driving east through Washington Park," a man once said, "and as soon as I passed Cottage Grove Avenue, I could tell from the deterioration that I was in a ward with an independent alderman." He was following the motto "Believing is seeing." The fact was that the Fifth Ward was in far better shape than almost any other ward in the city, because most Machine aldermen were primarily interested in acquiring patronage, office, or, in some cases, money.

Genuine attention to constituents built a strong body of supporters. In preparation for the 1963 election, the Fifth Ward Democratic Organization had sent out a scout to reconnoiter the Despres strength in Woodlawn, their longtime stronghold. The scout told me he returned with the message "He can't be beat."

Twenty Years Come to an End

20

I will only say that I have, with good intentions, contributed toward the organization and administration of the government the best exertions of which a very fallible judgment was capable.

George Washington, Farewell Address

To FILE or not to file—that was the question.

It was early November 1974. My twentieth year in office was drawing to a close. Nominating petitions for the next four-year term had to be filed in early December.

I decided to step aside and leave the field to others. The American people during my lifetime had decided that no matter how competent a president might be, he or she has to step aside after eight years. I had been in long enough. I was sixty-seven years old and in good health. I was swimming a half mile every morning. I concluded that I was ready to pursue different interests.

I thought about spending more effort on my law practice and engaging in nonpolitical pro bono work. I would still be working the equivalent of two jobs. I thought it might take just as much time as being alderman, but I would begin developing another side of my life.

No one stays in office indefinitely. There usually comes a day when the officeholder ceases to be reelected.

I prepared a statement announcing my intention. At an evening meeting in my home the day before I planned to release my decision, I disclosed it in confidence to my Fifth Ward Citizens Committee.

The committee members were friendly and sympathetic. They understood my position. They assured me of their support if I should choose to run.

One committee member quickly slipped out of the meeting and telephoned a friend to give him the information. He and his associates had been grooming a candidate should I not run. His action was tactless and a breach of confidence, but it strengthened my decision. People—at least some of them—were straining to back a new alderman.

In a few days, four male candidates appeared in a lively race: Al Raby, a remarkable civil rights advocate; Sidney Williams, a promising young anthropologist, the son of Sidney R. Williams of the Chicago Urban League; Ross Lathrop (who was elected), an employee of the University of Chicago; and Squire Lance, a former Woodlawn Organization director.

I decided to refrain scrupulously from taking part in the aldermanic campaign and held to it. The new person should test the electorate, I believed, and win on his own merits without support from me. All the candidates seemed to have maximum character qualifications, and I thought it would be no tragedy, whichever one were elected. In a way, Al Raby deserved the election for the remarkably good work he did over the years in fighting racial discrimination. Even so, I believed in the importance of each candidate's putting his own qualifications before the voters.

A group of my good supporters had circulated a petition with more than four thousand signatures asking me to reconsider and run again. I was deeply touched by their confidence, but resisted the temptation. I had already expressed myself against Mayor Daley's running again and said that in view of his health it would be the triumph of ego over prudence. He just could not give up. He did not last out his term, dying suddenly on December 20, 1976, at age seventy-four.

Leaving the city council meant leaving the arena where I had worked for so many years and had found colleagues of ability and temperament with whom working was an infinite satisfaction. At the head of the list, I mention Alderman William Cousins Jr. There is no one whose fortitude and character I admire more greatly. Aldermen Allen Freeman and John Hoellen were men with whom I could work effectively on problems of governmental efficiency and honesty.

There were three more aldermen of outstanding character and ability with whom it was a pleasure to work. They were Sammy Rayner Jr., Seymour Simon, and Dick Simpson. Alderman Simon was also a committeeman who some might say was tainted by patronage, but he was a person of such extraordinary ability, character, and independence that it was a joy to work with him. Dick Simpson has become the renowned historian of the city council and was an alderman of great distinction.

I felt wistful about not working with them again, but in the next city council only Alderman Dick Simpson would remain, although I was sure there would also be new aldermen of character with whom I could have forged alliances.

On the Daley side, I admired the abilities of a great many Machine aldermen, but they were inextricably dependent on the Machine. It takes a good deal of ability just to become an alderman. There were Machine aldermen of acumen, energy, and drive. Among them I had found only one whom I both admired and could work with constructively—William Murphy, the chairman of the Housing and Planning Committee when I entered the city council, and later a U.S. congressman. All those memories crowded on me when I made my announcement about not running again.

Reflection on the twenty years made me see the infinite debt I owed and still owe to the press. Despite limitations or complaints, we should be immensely grateful to the press, which enjoys such remarkable freedom in our country and city. Without it, I could not have achieved the things I did. I would simply have been a nonperson, and that would have been that. The press provided a court of appeal, a vehicle by which to reach out to the audience of readers and viewers so that what occurred in the city council was brought home to them. I often wanted fuller news stories, more explanation, greater elucidation, but the presence of a press was decisive in everything I accomplished.

At first, my relations with the press were tenuous. Some of the regular reporters assigned to city hall were skeptical of my interest, ability, or sincerity. As time went on, I was able to establish a credibility with them, which became invaluable.

Chicago newspapers had superb writers. Jay McMullen of the *Chicago Daily News* was one of them. His newspaper, in the tradition of Victor Lawson, allowed him to write fully about civic affairs. Bill Newman, also of the *Daily News*, was an outstanding writer.

Edward Schreiber of the *Tribune* was the paper's city hall reporter for all my twenty years. He had extraordinarily high standards of skepticism. Anything he wrote had to be accurate, significant, and, in his opinion, newsworthy. When he did write, his material was invaluable. On the *Sun-Times*, Harry Golden Jr. and on the late *Chicago Evening American*, Raymond McCarthy were splendid local reporters. All of them reported news about what happened in the city council and made it possible for me to raise and press issues.

In the *Chicago Daily News*, the *Chicago Sun-Times*, and later in the *Chicago Tribune*, the mordant, humorous columns of Mike Royko were invaluable when he turned his attention to the Chicago City Council.

I had no romance with the press. The reporters wrote what they considered newsworthy. On one occasion, in September 1958, when I attacked the housing provisions of the Hyde Park–Kenwood Urban Renewal Plan, the straight but dramatic press reports nearly lost me the ensuing election. The reporters were accurate. They conveyed the news story, and many constituents drew the impression that I wanted to kill urban renewal. It took me nearly six months and a bitter second election campaign to overcome what the press had done. Nevertheless, I could not complain of inaccuracy in their reporting.

Nothing had the impact of television. Someone said that a picture is worth a thousand words. That was a conservative estimate. When

Len O'Connor, an excellent television reporter, walked into the city council in 1960 during the police burglary crisis, and when the city council was thrown open to the television cameras and four or five cameras became regular attendants at all city council meetings, the effect was miraculous. There was no single essayist, no single writer, no single photographer who made such a difference. People could see and hear the highlights of city council meetings, with aldermen speaking for and against.

I have to pay special tribute to the *Hyde Park Herald*, a local newspaper owned by Bruce Sagan. As soon as I was elected alderman, he offered me the opportunity of writing a column in his paper. I wrote one for twenty years, and must have written more than eight or nine hundred columns headed "Your Alderman Reports." They provided a remarkable opportunity to communicate almost directly with constituents.

The *Hyde Park Herald* printed aldermanic news as it affected the local Hyde Park community and helped keep the constituents informed about me and me informed about them. I cannot overstate the importance of a conscientious local press in presenting editorial comment and news. In contrast, the Woodlawn community lacked a local newspaper.

In April 1975, I ended my twenty years in the city council.

Parliamentarian and Member of the Chicago Plan Commission

21

*Across the country and around the world, we've made it
clear that there's a new Spirit of Chicago, building on the old.*

Mayor Harold Washington, 1987 speech

Four years after I left the city council, I was sitting at the Sunday breakfast table when the telephone rang. It was Jane Byrne. Just that week she had been elected mayor of Chicago as a somewhat populist and somewhat anti-Machine champion.

"Would you be my parliamentarian in the city council?" she asked.

I was delighted, and accepted at once. It seemed to me an opportunity to renew contact with the city council and establish a relationship with the mayor.

At the first city council meeting, I took a seat in front of the rostrum where the mayor sat, just as the former parliamentarian had. When Mayor Daley assumed office in 1955, he had an excellent parliamentarian. He was an employee of the city clerk's office who attended each city council meeting until he died.

Mayor Daley himself was a formidable parliamentarian as a result of his years as a state senator and a party chairman. Throughout his twenty-one years as mayor of Chicago, he called for parliamentary advice only once, and then it was just for confirmation of his ruling. During Daley's administration, the parliamentarian died and was not replaced.

I assumed I would sit in his old chair. When Jane Byrne arrived to start the meeting, she said to me at once, "Come, sit up here, right next to me." I complied, and attended city council meetings for eight years thereafter, sitting first next to Mayor Byrne and then next to Mayor Harold Washington.

A good parliamentarian should follow a meeting closely and be prepared to rule at once on questions of proper procedure. Being parliamentarian was a glamorous employment, but it had nothing to do with directing or even participating in city policy. I was essentially an employee of the mayor.

Mayor Byrne needed me. She was inexperienced, pressured, and unfamiliar with plain *Robert's Rules of Order.* I had to assist her in elementary procedure and make sure that the city council meetings progressed smoothly.

As mayor, she proved a great disappointment. She entered office on a wave of popular support. Shortly after she began her term as mayor, she won a crucial city council vote over a core of Machine aldermen whom she had designated as an "evil cabal." After the vote was announced, the leader of the group, Alderman Vrdolyak, rose to say, "I know when I am beaten." This seemed to presage a strong administration with the mayor in full control of the city government and completely able to pursue the policies she had promised. But instead at the next meeting, she showed by her passivity she had made peace with the evil cabal.

From then on, she was more their captive than their executive. During city council meetings, aldermen used to approach the rostrum with slips of paper, which she would look at and place in her pocket for future action. I assumed they were requests for patronage or other favors, which she would dole out as an obedient mayor. She was left free to make appointments and was capricious in doing so.

Mayor Byrne loved to give parties generally at public expense and took a personal hand in making arrangements. As parliamentarian, I was invited. I remember with special delight the lavish parties for the president of Italy, the king and queen of Sweden, and, most elaborate of all, for the queen of Holland. Jane Byrne had the queen of Holland and herself transported by boat to the end of Navy Pier, where they disembarked to be greeted by twenty-four serenading violinists and a crowd of invited guests sipping Dom Perignon champagne.

She did change city policy to favor farmers' markets and outdoor cafes, but did not touch the city's basic problems. In a bold move, she identified with problems of housing segregation by herself moving into the almost all-black Cabrini Green, a public housing project, but she nullified her gesture by quickly moving out.

At the end of her term, after Washington announced that he would run, I strongly favored him. Although I tried to keep my public appearance as parliamentarian impartial, I did not succeed. She soon perceived where my support lay. Years later I chanced to meet her. Referring to my support of Washington, she said, "Remember me to your wife. She was always a help to me. That's more than I can say for you."

Just before her term expired, she gave a lavish party at Cricket's Restaurant, a fine Near North Side establishment. I said to her husband, Jay McMullen, "This is a wonderful party." He whispered in my ear, "I hope it ain't the last."

It was.

JANE BYRNE had appointed my wife to the Chicago Arts Council and appointed me to the Chicago Plan Commission, where I served from 1979 to 1989.

When Harold Washington was elected mayor in 1983, he continued to have the city employ me as parliamentarian, and I served until his death and the election of his successor. Harold Washington was the best mayor in Chicago's history. He was a voracious reader and an extremely well-informed person. He was personally identified with the social and economic problems of the city.

His need for a parliamentarian was something different from Jane Byrne's. He knew parliamentary law as well as the old mayor Daley.

What he required was someone on the rostrum with him who could help keep things moving and could direct his attention to the meeting when he was needed. He was so busy conferring with people who came up to talk to him that my function was to keep completely alert and notify him when his action had to be concentrated on the legislative body before him.

Under the G.I. Bill of Rights, Harold Washington had been a student of my wife's in social psychology at Roosevelt University. In after years, he always said when he saw her, "You started me on my political career."

What he referred to was her recommending to him that he run as a candidate for the student council. She had been impressed by his qualities of leadership and thought he would be a worthy representative. He ran, won, and was selected as president of the student council.

In fact, his political career began before that, when his father was a regular Democratic Party precinct captain and Harold had been exposed to all the machinations of such a captain. Nevertheless, from his postwar student days on, Harold Washington pursued a successful political career, and against Machine opposition. He was the opposite of Jane Byrne: concerned, decisive, and disdainful of the details of social party giving.

He asked me to preside at meetings and dinners, make speeches, and assist him in his inauguration ceremonies. In the first ceremony, I remember I recommended that he come down the aisle with Jane Byrne to take the oath of office. He sent word that he would not walk with Jane Byrne. He wanted to show that there was a clean break with what had come before. Working with him as parliamentarian was complete fun. I had a view of city council action that was unparalleled.

Washington reappointed me to the Chicago Plan Commission and toward the end designated me as vice chairman. I sat on the Chicago Plan Commission for ten years—years of complete frustration.

THE PLAN COMMISSION was a singularly powerless body. Except for matters arising under the Lakefront Protection Ordinance, virtually everything before the Plan Commission came under a statute that simply required the Plan Commission to look at the project. What the commission did was immaterial and unenforceable. Whether it approved, disapproved, or remained silent made no difference. At the end of thirty days, the proponents were free to go ahead. Consequently, the deliberations of the Plan Commission, however intelligent, were ineffectual both legally and practically. The *Chicago Tribune* city hall reporter, Edward Schreiber, called the Plan Commission deliberations mental masturbation.

The Lakefront Protection Ordinance, which was passed in 1973, delineated a narrow zone immediately abutting Lake Michigan and provided that nothing substantial could be built in it unless it met the grand purposes of the ordinance and won formal approval of the Plan Commission. There the Plan Commission had some power, but I recall only one significant matter under the Lakefront Protection Ordinance in all my ten years on the commission.

For the bulk of the work, the presentation was worked out in private between the developer and the Department of Planning and then showcased for public display. The Plan Commission itself had no staff. The Department of Planning worked under the direction of the mayor. The mayors were all developer minded. Byrne used to love ground-breaking and topping-off ceremonies for new buildings. Washington wanted to show, I believe, that construction of new buildings could continue under a nonwhite mayor.

When a project came before the Plan Commission for its approval or disapproval, we would generally receive a report from a traffic expert, a description from an architect, and a report from some other expert, and that would generally be the end. Any objectors were courteously allowed to speak, and then the matter was put to a vote. The other members of the Plan Commission had adopted the principle "Let 'em build."

In addition, the fact that nearly all matters were presented by the Department of Planning meant that the mayor favored them. Over and over I would point out that a project would fatally add to density. Unfortunately there were no planning principles effectively adopted by the city against which to judge a project. I would ask, "Are we to approve congestion so that we won't be able to move?" The answer would always be yes. Today in many parts of the Loop and the North Side and especially in Streeterville, an elite residential section of the North Side, there are many times when vehicular traffic is almost unable to move. My questions and my objections had no effect. The approval would, as someone said, "Sail through like a hot wind off the desert." There was no discussion of conflicting goals, because there were no planning goals to discuss. I'm sure that the planning department, particularly under Mayor Washington and department head Elizabeth Hollander, eked out all the "marginal amenities" it could. We have, for example, street-level stores and reduced height that she and her staff were able to obtain as concessions, but once a matter was completed and presented to the Plan Commission, it sailed through.

Just once under the Lakefront Protection Ordinance there was a genuine conflict. In 1985, the developers asked for relaxation of the height restriction for a high building at 600 North Lake Shore Drive, at the corner of Ohio Street. The testimony showed that the proposed skyscraper would cast its 5:00 p.m. shadow all the way to Navy Pier by late June. By October the shadow would reach across the lake's inlet, across Olive Park, and all the way to the central water filtration plant. The skyscraper would obstruct views of the lake from other apartment and office towers. It would choke the area. This was one proposal that needed an affirmative vote of the Plan Commission in order to proceed.

It was not a case where it made no difference what the Plan Commission did. The commission was so pro-developer that the only votes against the project were from Elizabeth Hollander and me.

The ridiculous argument was made that by allowing the building to reach this outrageous height, the city would be "democratizing the lakefront." At so many dollars per apartment!

On two occasions I tried to commit the Plan Commission to modest planning goals for the city, once through a written subcommittee report on parking lots in the Loop area and another time by a statement of the commission's policy on the lakefront. My efforts were politely received and that was all.

During my ten years I could not find a fellow commissioner who was interested in planning. Consequently I finally came to the conclusion that it would be wise for me to give up my membership on the commission.

Neither as parliamentarian nor as member of the Plan Commission did I have the power of an elected alderman to shape city policy.

City Watchdog Calling It Quits

Leon Despres to End Ten Years on Plan Commission

James Warren, *Chicago Tribune*, January 3, 1989

I⊤ MAY be lonely at the top, but Leon Despres knows better of the solitude at the bottom and fringe. Now, he's stepping aside from an honorable, nettlesome role of prickly dissenter.

Despres, 80, the former independent Hyde Park alderman from 1955 to 1975 who fought often with Mayor Richard J. Daley, is quietly cutting his last formal tie to city government.

On Tuesday, the city Planning Department will receive a one-line letter, informing them that Despres is quitting the Chicago Plan Commission, a body meant to make sure that zoning changes are in the city's best interest and to have final say on anything built within three blocks of Lake Michigan.

Elizabeth Hollander, the city planning commissioner, was surprised Monday when informed of the impending move. "He's raised a lot of questions for which we need good answers. He will be missed."

Despres has served on the nine-member commission since 1979, when he was appointed by Mayor Jane Byrne. He was reappointed by Mayor Harold Washington. Between 1979 and 1987, he was parliamentarian for the City Council, a position he left shortly after the death of Washington and the selection of Eugene Sawyer as acting mayor.

The Plan Commission is meant to be a tough-minded overseer, but it has tended to function as more of a rubber stamp for the wishes of the administration in power. Time and again, Despres has been a minority of one in debates over building a commercial tower here or a big residential complex there—a minority viewpoint when the commission opts for condos rather than a small park or changes a zoning requirement to assist a builder.

"This has been a developer's decade," Despres said. "The commission is supposed to be a body of some independence and originality, but hasn't been that at all."

Despres usually has refused to agree with deals in which the city bends or waives a rule in return for an arcade, a shop, a few more parking spaces. He's rarely bought the notion that development and jobs are justifications for buildings that, he feels, result in overcrowding and gridlock.

An admirable purist to some, a cantankerous scold and doctrinaire nay-sayer to many others, he's been indefatigable, especially in raising questions about what the city might be giving away in a deal.

"Citizens should be concerned about the commission due to problems of protecting neighborhoods, the lakefront and manufacturing, and with the saturation and overcrowding," Despres said. "Unfortunately, there's always tremendous pressure on mayors to show development and showy buildings, especially in the central district."

HOLLANDER, whose personal politics mesh more often than not with those of Despres, frequently was at odds with him.

"Often, I think his positions have been somewhat extreme," she said. "He's more against density than I am. He'd like to have more planning and with that I don't disagree. His point of view has been to articulate an alternative view. As in the City Council, it's often been a lone view."

Despres called Hollander "the best planning commissioner we've had . . . completely honorable and with high standards. But her position requires her to be pragmatic and steer a course among good planning, the wishes of the mayor and those of the council."

RECENT issues, big and small, typify the Despres perspective:

- The commission approved a plan to build a 29-story office tower in the Streeterville neighborhood east of Michigan Avenue and north of the Chicago River, allowing the developer to build four extra floors but without requiring pedestrian arcades that are normally a part of such a "density bonus."

  Despres said the deal exemplified the need to rewrite the zoning code to assure the city getting needed amenities.

- The commission approved Loyola University's plan to build a landfill to enlarge its Rogers Park campus. Despres was the lone dissenter, saying,

"The basic policy of the city is and should continue to be that Chicago's priceless asset, Lake Michigan and the lakefront, are not for sale."
- Despres criticized expansion of the Chicago Historical Society and Shedd Aquarium and development of Meigs Field. "It was an unfortunate accident that Meigs Field was ever created in the first place," he said. "It provided a comfortable landing place for a few people or businesses that were rich enough to have planes. It should be phased out."
- Despres voted against the development of another giant office building adjacent to the Sears Tower. The commission granted developers extra density for the proposed 65-story Sears Franklin Center in return for sidewalk arcades that won't be built and a pair of pedestrian tunnels that might be. He had voted against plans for three 60-story towers on the block immediately south of the tower.

Commission member Doris Holleb conceded Monday the public's view of Despres as a man of "ramrod integrity. He has a sophisticated sensibility for corruption and cronyism. He can sniff it out like a bloodhound."

But Holleb said he has rubbed even potential confederates the wrong way, with a mix of absolutism on issues and condescension in tone. "He'll stake out what he considers the high ground and everybody else is a moral pygmy," she said.

As DESPRES was adding a handwritten note to his typed resignation, he sat back from his desk and said: "Developers are always hungry to overexploit a situation. That doesn't mean that every developer is bad. But if you have rules to equalize opportunities, you're better off."

His legacy after 10 years? "Well, I regret I couldn't do a little more, though I think I've had some accomplishments. If I had any allies, I wouldn't want to let them down. As it is, I have friends on the commission, but no allies."

The Most Segregated City in the North— Chicago

Leon M. Despres, *Chicago Scene*, February 15, 1962

As Chicago school segregation moves toward a court showdown, the sordid history of segregation is again in the limelight.

Chicago, in 1962, has the largest Negro residential area of any city in the United States. Nearly all of Chicago's 813,000 Negro citizens live in one continuous T-shaped area which stretches from the Indiana State line to Chicago's downtown, then across the western part of the near north side, and finally west from downtown almost to the city line. This enormous area has become Chicago's Negro ghetto, a huge Black Metropolis, incorporating nearly all the former enclaves which used to provide population dispersion. Except for Hyde Park-Kenwood and a very few other neighborhoods, Chicago now has nothing resembling stable interracial communities.

In 1948, Robert Weaver, the present Housing and Home Finance Administrator, wrote in *The Negro Ghetto* that Chicago had already "become the most completely segregated area in the industrial North." In 1959, the United States Civil Rights Commission found that "in terms of racial residential patterns, Chicago is the most segregated city of more than 500,000 in the country." Chicago's housing segregation is steadily growing more severe. In fact, it has become the single most important factor hampering Chicago's development as a great city.

Other northern cities practice residential segregation, but none so systematically as Chicago. People ask how this happened to Chicago, about which the Indians used to say, referring to Jean Baptiste Point du Sable, "The first white settler in Chicago was a Negro!" It happened as a result of Chicago's savage anti-Negro repression from 1917 to 1921 and the Chicago Rule of Segregation imposed in 1917 and lasting to this day.

Until the Great Migration of 1915 to 1918, Chicago had a small Negro population, much of it dispersed throughout the entire city. In 1910, 44,000 Negro residents made up 2 percent of the population, and more than half of them lived outside the small Black Belt.

During the Great Migration Chicago's industrial requirements attracted badly-needed Negro rural labor. In one eighteen-month period alone, Chicago received more than 50,000 southern Negroes. Like the earlier rural in-migrants, the new Negroes moved into old areas near the center of Chicago, especially the Black Belt on the South Side where they found the supporting presence of other recent arrivals with the same background.

So many Negroes came to Chicago during the Great Migration that even after they filled every cranny in the Black Belt, they still had to look desperately for homes, just at the time when the war had stopped residential buildings. Inevitably, they began to push the Black Belt outward along its edges with the first great expansion southward on South Parkway.

From 1917 on, official and unofficial Chicago dealt very harshly with the residential needs of Negro Chicagoans. In that year, a committee of the all white Chicago Real Estate Board laid down Chicago's Rule of Segregation, which has been substantially followed up to the present: "The old districts are overflowing and new territory must be furnished. . . . It is desired in the interest of all, that each block shall be filled solidly and that further expansion shall be confined to contiguous blocks, and that the present method of obtaining a single building in scattered blocks be discontinued. Promiscuous sales and leases here and there mean an unwarranted and unjustifiable destruction of values . . . In the fact of existing conditions the Committee has in an unprejudiced spirit reached the above conclusion and hopes for active cooperation from all civic bodies."

The request for "active cooperation" was met. From July 1, 1917 to March 1, 1921, white Chicagoans enforced the Rule of Segregation by systematically bombing an average of one home every twenty days. Most of the bombed homes belonged to Negroes outside the Black Belt. Some homes belonged to white persons who had sold homes to Negroes, or said they would, or simply helped Negroes buy a home.

So precise was the bombing policy that in 1922 the Chicago Race Relations Commission was able to report: "News of threatened bombings in many cases was circulated well in advance of the actual occurrence. Negroes were warned of the exact date on which explosions would occur. They asked for police protection, and, in some instances where police were sent beforehand, their homes were bombed, and no arrests were made."

So strong was Chicago's official and unofficial approval that during the entire period the authorities did not obtain one bombing indictment, lodged only one charge, and obtained no conviction.

In the midst of the bombing campaign, Chicago used an "episode of brief, sudden, and massive terror" to provide a decisive reenforcement of residential segregation. After a clash at the Twenty-ninth Street beach, white gangs and "athletic clubs" took advantage of the incident to whip up feelings. They roamed the Black Belt from July 27 to August 2, 1919, and committed acts of murder, injury, pillage, and fire. The dead were thirty-eight, 23 Negroes and 15 whites; the injured, 537; homes burned or pillaged, uncounted. Photographs of lynching, burnings, and violence were available. The authorities knew many of the killers, perhaps most of them. Nevertheless, the Chicago police and the State's Attorney's office indicted only nine people and convicted four—two white and two Negro.

The repression took effect, and Chicago's Negro community found itself hemmed in more tightly than any Negro community in any other large northern city. From 1917 on, expansion of the segregated area followed the rule laid down by the Chicago Real Estate Board: "If you must expand, you are to do so just as slowly as possible."

Physical violence against residential expansion continued. In fact, it is continuing even now at the regular rate of two and three incidents a month. There are even occasional bombings. One residential dynamite bombing occurred, for example, on January 12, 1962, because a Negro bought a house in a white block on S. Union Avenue. After 1921, the previous scale of physical violence was no longer necessary. The unforgettable memories of past terror, the regular monthly incidents, and occasional dramatic reminders such as the outbreaks at Trumbull Park and Cicero in the 1950's have been quite enough to force Negroes and whites to follow the Rule of Segregation.

In addition to physical violence, Chicago white real estate interests began a new approach in the 1920's—the racial restrictive covenant. The covenant was a mutual written agreement among property owners in a given area, by which each signer agreed not to sell or lease his property to a Negro and not let a Negro live on it except as a bona fide house servant. For 25 years, local associations, large landowners, and professional advocates pushed the covenant campaign. As a result, racial covenants blanketed the properties around Negro residential areas, sterilized suburbs and subdivisions, and directly affected, it was said, as much as 80 percent of all white residential property in Chicago. In case of covenant violations, Chicago courts regularly issued injunctions and enforced them.

The covenants were a powerful segregation weapon. They slowed up peripheral expansion of the ghetto when it did finally occur, and they forbade nonsegregated expansion. Toward the end of their 25 year life, legal chinks began to appear. For example, the courts found a technical reason to strike down covenants on the properties just south of Washington Park. Generally, the covenants were enforced until 1948, when the United States Supreme Court held that they were unenforceable. Even today they are not completely dead. The Chicago Title and Trust Company still dutifully shows racial covenants on its title guaranty policies. "The Supreme Court said they were unenforceable," explained a title officer, "but did not say they were void!"

Besides physical violence and racial covenants, Chicago also used direct and overwhelming economic pressure. Since the time of the Great Migration, people who have violated the Rule of Segregation have repeatedly suffered severe economic reprisals—no financing, no insurance protection, no tenants, no income. Brokers, managers, owners, inspectors, private and public financing agencies, and even local governments have worked to preserve Chicago's Rule of Segregation. Persistent violators have quite simply been ruined.

The first change in official Chicago's attitude toward residential violence came during World War II. Like World War I, World War II brought to Chicago another large migration of needed southern Negro labor, another suspension of residential building, and then more pressure to expand the ghetto at the edges. After World War II, Chicago's industries boomed, and the in-migration continued. It was under Mayor Kelly that the city government first began to provide substantial police protection for move-ins at the ghetto edges.

Under Mayors Kelly and Kennelly, another change occurred for a time. The Chicago Housing Authority began to follow a policy of locating new public housing projects on available land throughout the city, and then, after the new housing was built, gradually developing interracial tenancies. This simple policy produced such an extraordinary explosion, as at Trumbull Homes, that the state changed the law and forced the Housing Authority to submit all new public housing sites to the City Council before going ahead. Under the new law, the aldermen have approved no family public housing sites outside the segregated area. In fact, some of the older public housing projects outside the ghetto are still lily-white or nearly so. Bridgeport Homes, for example, has no Negro occupants.

Today, although the legally enforceable racial covenant is gone and physical violence is less terrible than it used to be, economic pressure and steady violence keep Chicago a segregated city. The city government does protect slow expansion around the ghetto's edges, but takes no leadership in changing the segregation pattern. The Chicago Rule of Segregation still prevails. In 1959, Mayor Daley explained simply but disingenuously to the United States Civil Rights Commission: "We are constantly running into difficult problems."

The suburbs are worse. They are a "white noose" around the city. They are lily white except for a few isolated cases: publicized cases such as Dr. Arthur Falls in Western Springs and Dr. Percy Julian in Oak Park; some unpublicized cases; a few Negro suburbs such as Robbins; a few segregated enclaves as in Evanston; and Negro servants. Out of every 1,000 newspaper advertisements for new houses in a "Chicagoland model community," 999 carry the unwritten but clear admonition: "No Negroes need apply."

Some parts of the Black Metropolis in Chicago are attractive, spacious and well maintained. Recently, Channel 2 showed block after block of upper middle class single family homes on the far south side of the segregated area, west of Cottage Grove. To an uninformed white person who equates "Negro and poor housing," these attractive homes are very impressive. They show that high property values, good maintenance, and the presence of Negroes are compatible. They show that Negro Chicagoans have the same aspirations as white Chicagoans, and that among Negroes as well as whites, high-status groups tend to be residentially separated from low-status groups. Nevertheless, even the high-status Negro area is part of the ghetto and subject to its pressures and restraints.

What Chicago's housing segregation does to the people inside the segregated area is unbelievable. It imposes segregated institutions and facilities of all kinds—churches, social organizations, restaurants, barber shops, taverns, stores, transportation, amusements, and social intercourse. It produces overcrowded and segregated schools with the consequence of inferior schooling. It isolates Chicago color groups from each other. It perpetuates handicaps. It causes terrible overcrowding in most portions of the ghetto area—five times the average density outside—with the consequent overuse of land and buildings. It uses old buildings that are unfit, and makes new buildings old before their time. It allows Chicago landlords, both Negro and white, to gouge their tenants. It forces ghetto residents, who already suffer employment discrimination, to pay just as much rent per family as white Chicagoans, but for less good accommodations, and out of much lower average incomes.

After paying rent, an average Chicago Negro family has much less money available than the average white family, for food, clothing, education, medical care, and all the other necessities and amenities of life. To add to the deprivations, our local governments—city, school board, and park district— give to the segregated area the least good schools, the lowest per capita recreation facilities, the poorest police protection, and the poorest municipal services. The school board passively follows a "neighborhood" school policy, i.e. it simply accepts residential segregation as a foundation for schooling.

Worst of all, Chicago's residential segregation does something severe to individual and group personalities. "Some of the effects can be seen with the eye," says Father Hesburgh, former chairman of the United States Civil Rights Commission. "Some can be shown by statistics. Some can be measured in the mind and heart." Chicago's housing segregation creates a terrifying crucible which does, it is true, refine some souls of steel, and Chicago will be inordinately proud of the poets, artists, philosophers, scientists, and public leaders who survive the crucible. But on most residents of the area, the crucible inflicts debilitating injuries which never heal.

To Chicagoans of African descent, Chicago has done something it never did to any other arrivals. The Chicago descendants of European immigrants, as they proved their abilities and exercised their choice, have been allowed the option of moving out of the immigrant neighborhoods and into multigroup middle and upper class white neighborhoods. But the Chicago descendants of African immigrants, no matter how educated, wealthy, accomplished, urbane, moral, or law-abiding—with the exception of those few who live in an island of hope such as Hyde Park-Kenwood and Lake Meadows—must remain forever in the segregated area. There is also housing discrimination against Chicagoans of Jewish and Asian ancestry, but it is not comparable in extent or ferocity with the segregation of Negro Chicagoans.

Segregation is also a heavy and cruel burden on the white Chicagoan outside the ghetto area. It coarsens him, forces him to rely on violence and subterfuge, isolates him from his fellow Chicagoans, unfits him for life in a world that is two-thirds nonwhite, and deceives him into reliance on segregation as a way to preserve his neighborhood community. It encourages white Chicagoans to neglect renewal, rehabilitation, and far-sighted planning; and to make violent racial stands at viaducts, boulevards, parks, expressways, or other supposed barriers, until the population pressure breaks through, somehow, to some extent.

Chicago's segregation creates a vicious circle, which Myrdal's *American Dilemma* describes perfectly: "When a few Negro families do come into a white neighborhood, some more white families move away. Other Negroes hasten to take their places, because the existing Negro neighborhoods are overcrowded due to segregation. This constant movement of Negroes into white neighborhoods makes the bulk of the white residents feel that their neighborhood is doomed to be predominantly Negro, and they move out—with their attitudes against the Negro reinforced. Yet if there were no segregation, this wholesale invasion would not have occurred. But because it does occur, segregational attitudes are increased, and the vigilant pressure to stall the Negroes at the borderline is kept up."

Segregation withers communities around the edges of the expanding ghetto. Once you have seen a Chicago community crumble under the effects of segregation, you never forget it. The white Chicagoan who keeps his racial prejudices grows more bitter. The white Chicagoan who sees that it was not "the Negro" but segregation that caused the tragedy, gains insight and realization that it is segregation that must go.

If you want to see the process in operation, walk, cycle, or slowly drive down a street inside the ghetto (say south on Carpenter or Union), and follow it to the edge of the ghetto and beyond. Look at the mixed blocks, then the blocks dotted with "For Sale" signs, then the quiet and fearful white blocks, then the white blocks which will be directly affected only next year or the year after. You will see with your own eyes the amazing internal migration which, between 1950 and 1960, gave Chicago more Negroes and 400,000 fewer whites, and you will see the work of the "blockbusters," who carry out Chicago's Rule of Segregation and fatten on it.

As the Chicago ghetto inevitably expands, many white people often decide that they will not flee, but will judge each neighbor as an individual and will remain. Tragically, however, if the ghetto expands and if thoughtless whites do flee, the pressures of overcrowding bring ghetto conditions to the area, and tend to make the surviving white residents move away, one by one, as they experience the results of overcrowding and segregation in the streets, schools, community facilities, and churches. They finally decide to exercise their option to move. No such option is available to the Negro Chicagoan. He must bear the overcrowding which the white Chicagoan can avoid.

Housing segregation has become the number one enemy of Chicago's urban progress. It has emasculated Chicago's urban renewal, because it makes so many white Chicagoans interpret nondiscrimination in governmental urban renewal to mean Negro inundation; or they fear that the demolition which accompanies urban renewal will force displaced Negroes to reenter the ghetto and thus increase the pressure at the edges. Segregation makes many Negro Chicagoans fear urban renewal because the same demolitions diminish the total housing supply available to Negroes and increase the competition for what is left.

For all Chicago, segregation forces low housing standards, impaired home life, mounting juvenile delinquency, and other contagious social pathology and decay which cross all barriers and outpace any possible urban renewal program for Chicago.

Who gains from Chicago's segregation? More than anyone else, the real estate owners inside the segregated area. They enjoy a landlord's bonus, a Chicago color tax which averages fifteen dollars per dwelling unit, a rent differential which the Negro dwelling finances by intensive use of space. The color tax made the 1960 average monthly rent in segregated Woodlawn, for example, forty dollars a room! Real estate manipulators profit from housing segregation. Chicagoans, both Negro and white, have made fortunes buying low from panic-ridden whites and selling high to segregation-ridden Negroes. Demagogues gain from segregation.

Chicago as a whole, both white and nonwhite, simply cannot afford to continue residential segregation. In 1950, 492,000 Chicagoans were segregated. In 1960, 813,000. In 1970? In 1980? As Chicagoans sit back, Chicago grows *more* segregated, not less. In the midst of inaction, sweet pleas for gradualism and rosy predictions of progress are just cloaks for inaction.

If Chicagoans (including suburban Chicagoans) could fully understand the costs and consequences of Chicago's residential segregation, they would speedily bring it to an end. They would soon provide laws, ordinances, leadership, and dispersions. Negro Chicagoans, like all other Chicagoans, would then live where their tastes, abilities, and personal achievements permit. The arrival of Negro neighbors would no longer mean that an inundation would follow. Chicago's true period of greatness could then begin.

It is high time for Chicago to repeal the 1917 Chicago Rule of Segregation and move toward urban greatness. It has the necessary resources. It has the tradition of the world's greatest melting pot. Chicago needs only to decide: "We will."

The Lone "Negro" Spokesman in Chicago's City Council

David Llorens, *Negro Digest*, December 1966

IRONICALLY enough, it was just prior to Chicago's West Side up-rising and Martin Luther King's assault on Chicago's segregated neighborhoods that the agenda for a City Council meeting included an ordinance to approve 11 public housing sites. Each of them in Negro neighborhoods.

A lean, professorial looking alderman spoke to the matter.

> In view of the present condition of this ordinance, it ought to be defeated. It proposes four intolerable family high-rise buildings which our experience has demonstrated to be harmful. . . . It is bad city policy and bad civil rights policy. Since public housing is non-discriminatory, it says that anyone who wants to live in public housing will have to live inside the segregated Negro area, and that no non-discriminatory public housing will be allowed in the white ghetto outside the segregated Negro area.
>
> And what is proposed today is the counterpart of the policy we discussed at the last City Council meeting, when we considered the actions of high city officials who lead the government and public opinion and reside in buildings and belong to clubs which have rigid barriers against both Negro and Jewish Americans. . . .

"Point of order, Mr. President," cried a short, stocky alderman. "This is irrelevant and flag-waving. It has nothing to do with the 11 sites we are considering."

"The point of order is well taken," spoke the chairman, who happened to be Chicago Mayor Richard J. Daley. The first alderman appealed the order from the chair on the ground that it would be suppression of highly relevant discussion. The chair was sustained, with one dissenting vote.

Perhaps the little drama will not seem unfamiliar to those acquainted with debates concerning the urban Negro taking place throughout the nation's large Northern cities. But Chicagoans think their situation is unique?

The lean alderman, who called passage of the ordinance "a naked display of white power," is Leon M. Despres. His antagonist, who usually finds Despres' efforts on behalf of Chicago's Negro population "irrelevant," is Alderman Claude W. Holman. Despres is white. Holman is Black.

But Alderman Holman—along with five other Negro aldermen—is a member of the Cook County Democratic Party, better known as the "Daley Machine," and Alderman Despres is an independent Democrat, not accountable to the mayor who also is the chairman of the Cook County Democratic Central Committee.

Leon M. Despres was born in Chicago in 1908, and has lived in the Fifth Ward—the ward he has represented since 1955—since he was a small boy. The Fifth Ward consists of a large part of the integrated Hyde Park community and most of Woodlawn, home of one of the nation's strongest community organizations, The Woodlawn Organization, a neighborhood where few but the merchants are white.

While political action chairman of the liberal IVI (Independent Voters of Illinois), and engaged in private law practice, Despres was asked by fellow IVI members to run for alderman. Elected in 1955, and reelected in 1959 and in a bitterly contested battle in 1963, his opposition to the Daley Machine in matters of racial policy has become more vehement over the years, rather paralleling the mood of the total Negro community.

When asked how he feels about being labeled "rebel" and "maverick" by Chicago newspapers, Despres smiles slightly, and says, "Well, I guess it means I do not accept a very undesirable *status quo.*"

A motion resolution or amendment introduced before the city council by Alderman Despres is almost invariably the prologue to a ritual, usually beginning with a repudiation by Alderman Holman (and frequently joined by other administration aldermen) whose remarks often approach the point of insult. Despres candidly states: "Holman responds to me on assignment from Daley and Keane (Alderman Thomas E. Keane is the administration floor leader)." And the epilogue to the ritual seldom changes. Despres-sponsored measures are usually tabled, sent to committee, or defeated outright.

To critics who contend that Despres could accomplish more as a member of the regular democratic organization (the Machine) rather than as its chief antagonist, he replies, "I could certainly (as an organization man) be more effective in terms of patronage and favors, but less effective in matters of policy." His independency, insists Despres, allows him the freedom to advocate his viewpoints. "Administration aldermen can't talk or introduce anything without permission."

The outspoken alderman contends that he has more influence on the basic issue of integration because, "through bringing up issues, I can compel the Machine to take a position," and he adds, "though they won't give me credit."

Despres cites, for example, his having introduced early in 1965 an amendment to the city's elevator code, after four Woodlawn children were killed as a result of mechanical failures of elevators. The amendment, which called for stronger elevator safety requirements, was defeated. However, sometime later, the administration—on orders from Mayor Daley, says Despres—introduced an identical amendment, which became law.

To the six Negro administration aldermen—often called "the silent six"—politics means "jobs, status and money," says Despres. He thinks that because they are Negroes they cannot fail to understand the problem of segregation and oppression. But the Fifth Ward alderman, who was supported in his 1963 campaign against a Negro attorney by such prominent Chicago Negroes as Earl B. Dickerson and Truman K. Gibson Sr., as well as by the city's civil rights leaders, thinks that the six Negroes are less responsive to the needs of the Negro community "because they are in the business of living off politics—I am not."

Exactly what is the business of living off politics? "The political Machine dominates the Negro vote," says Despres, "with its mercenary army of patronage jobs, from which a man is fired at once if he fails to perform his political work." For most of those holding the same 35,000 political jobs controlled by the "Machine," the political work is precinct work—delivering the vote. A former political appointee, Leahmon L. Reid, now a newsman, comments that it was not unusual for one who was reported to be "not out ringing doorbells"—which was not a part of his "official" duties—to be admonished, "You're not doing anything for the party!"

According to Despres, in addition to delivering the vote, political work might involve such things as "control of the local NAACP." He also accuses the "mercenary army" of miscounting, padding and buying elections.

Despres thinks political organization is a necessity for civil rights-minded groups, but he contends that infiltrating the Machine is impossible. "If you stay in the Machine very long," he says, "it infiltrates you." The Machine is completely autocratic, says the alderman. "The ward committeeman appoints everyone and can remove anyone he wants removed." There are approximately 500 political patronage jobs available to each ward, and the ward committeemen, who include five of the six Negro aldermen, are directly accountable to chairman Daley.

Commenting on the widely publicized fact that Mayor Daley does not tolerate much dissension within his ranks, Despres maintains that "any adulation of Daley short of idolatry is considered treason," but he facetiously adds, "Daley is not a dictator—he's more like the president of a corporation."

LEON M. DESPRES, affectionately called "Len" by business associates and friends, has consistently pleased civil rights advocates with his positions. He was one of the leaders in the effort to oust controversial School Superintendent Benjamin C. Willis, described by Despres as "a man whose entire life has been devoted to hatred." The Fifth Ward reformist has attempted, in vain, to push through stronger legislation on open occupancy. He has been a familiar figure in civil rights marches in Chicago, as well as having made the journey to Selma in the Spring of 1965. A strong Despres resolution supporting the move to withhold the seats of Mississippi congressmen challenged by the Mississippi Freedom Democratic Party was defeated in favor of a weaker administration motion.

One of the more illustrious examples of the battling alderman in action was, perhaps, a seven hour debate over James Baldwin's *Another Country*, in which he led the opposition to the administration's attempt to ban the novel from a required reading list in a course at one of the city's public junior colleges. Moreover, the session provided insight into the peculiar situation of the administration's Negro councilmen.

Despres, especially eloquent in his defense of academic freedom and author James Baldwin, equated "Chicago's Tammany" with Moscow's Kremlin for its censorship efforts, and called the book banning venture "an attempt to discredit Baldwin because he is a Negro writer."

The six Negro aldermen sat silently throughout the session, but during a recess, one of them, Alderman Robert H. Miller, told a reporter, "The city council has no jurisdiction in this matter." He further commented on the "ridiculousness" of the effort. But when the time came to vote on a resolution requiring the Board of Education to remove the book from the required reading list, Alderman Miller, as did the other organization men, voted to ban the novel. The resolution, however, later provided futile.

The session over Baldwin's novel pointed up the intellectual acumen (which appears rather an anomaly in the city's legislative body) of Leon Despres.

Chicago reporter Sam Blair once noted that Despres' use of polysyllabic words during a council presentation, while capturing the interest of high school observers left the other aldermen puzzled. Despres, a man given to research, can be seen taking notes during council sessions with a youthful zest that belies his 58 years. Both his demeanor and scholarship are in radical contrast to that of his chamber adversaries whose staidness would defy even the ancient Roman courts.

The alderman does not reject the label "intellectual," but reminds one, "But that does not mean that I am without human warmth or compassion."

As a critic of Mayor Daley, Despres is invective. He thinks the mayor would prefer that city council never meet, and maintains that all the decisions are made "in Daley's inner councils." Laughingly, he speaks of the administration aldermen's desperation to make themselves heard: "Often, at the opening of a council meeting, as many as 20 aldermen will read long speeches memorializing a deceased city figure—they're real good at talking about dead men."

Despres holds Daley responsible for the perpetuation of both housing and school segregation. He contends that Daley, while using the national Democratic image and political patronage to hold the Negro vote, "has catered to the segregationist vote by supporting the pattern of segregation. . . ."

He thinks the mayor is threatened by the presence of Martin Luther King Jr., explaining that the white community will react against the mayor if he is unable to contain civil rights activity, such as marches in the white community. "White segregationists become angry at people who thwart their hatred," says Despres. Although the six Negro aldermen have consistently praised the mayor as a champion of Negro rights, Despres, without hesitation, states: "Daley is at heart, and by personal conduct, a white segregationist."

More often than not, Despres opposes the mayor's appointments, from those to the school board and library board to the mayor's choice for director of the city's Commission on Human Relations.

"The commission," says Despres, "acts as midwife to the growth of the ghetto," and of its director, Ed Marciniak, one of Daley's highly touted appointees, "Everyone knew that he was chosen to do the kind of job the mayor wanted done—essentially a political cover up."

The usually quick-speaking alderman answers a bit slower when asked about Black Power, which he finds an "elusive term." Despres believes the integrationists can "save" the city. "If you know anything about the conditions in the United States, you understand the notions of Black Power. I've never joined with those who denounce the Muslims—whose headquarters are in my ward—which doesn't mean I join them, but I understand them." Segregation, says Despres, "can destroy the city."

He thinks whites should not expect special gratitude or favors for speaking out on behalf of the Negro, and asserts that "you can't fully end oppression until the oppressed have complete freedom to express themselves."

The alderman, described by Chicago novelist Ronald Fair as the "only 'Negro' in city government," foresees the cracking of the Daley Machine. "The place to break the Machine," says Despres, "is the Democratic primary— *as an independent.*" In the June primary this year, a significant breakthrough to that effect was made. Two independent Negro candidates beat the Democratic Machine for the Illinois Senatorial candidacy, and both were expected to beat their Republican opposition in November.

Some of Despres' positions over the past two years have drawn strong criticism from some of the predominantly white Hyde Park community organizations, as well as the University of Chicago administration (which is located in his ward). Does he expect that this factor, along with the heightened cry for Black political power, will hinder him in next Spring's election?

"I've lost a little section of white support," he says, without a trace of worry, "but I've gained enough Negro and white votes to offset the loss."

No matter what side one takes on the racial issue, it is pretty generally agreed in Chicago that when an issue supported by civil rights advocates comes before Chicago's city council, one man can be counted on to speak and vote in its favor. But it seems so natural. After all, Leon M. Despres usually introduces such issues.

Excerpts from "A Report on City of Chicago Employment Discrimination against Women"

Prepared by Arlene Selvern and Margaret Hughes under the direction of Alderman Leon M. Despres, June 29, 1972

The purpose of this study is to indicate the broad extent of the Chicago City Government's employment discrimination against women, and to recommend broad and urgent remedies. From general observation we had long known of the employment discrimination. The actual figures we found, in ten departments chosen as random samples, are a disgrace to the city. We have divided this report into the following sections:

1. What We Studied and How We Did It.
2. The Specific Constitutional and Legal Obligations of the City Not to Discriminate. What the Study Showed as to Discrimination in Ten City Departments.
3. What the City Should Do about It at Once.
4. What Citizens Can Do about It.

1. What We Studied and How We Did It

Although we would have liked to present a study covering all city employees, the results to date are so startling, and the time requirement for a total investigation is so long under the working conditions imposed by the Mayor and the Civil Service Commission, that we believe this report should be published now. The broad sample we are presenting raises so many grave questions about the city's employment practices that, without delay, we believe they should be fully answered and the city's employment discrimination against women should be ended. We examined the Civil Service Commission printout payrolls of the following departments:

Department	Number of Employees
Buildings	686
Civil Service Commission	132
Development and Planning	95
Environmental Control	147
Finance	374
Human Resources	374
Law	250
Mayor's Office	93
Municipal Tuberculosis Sanitarium	732
Purchases, Contracts, and Supplies	237
Total	3,120

These printout payroll sheets were made available to us under Municipal Code Section 25–29 which provides:

> All departments, bureaus, boards or persons connected with the city government are hereby required to make such financial reports as may be ordered by the city council, and to permit examination of all their official records by any member of the city council, or any accredited representative of the press, except such records which by law are required to be kept confidential or which by ordinance are limited to inspection by certain designated persons.

However, under orders of the Mayor, the Civil Service Commission refused to let us take the printout sheets with us or even photocopy them. Therefore, Arlene Selvern and Margaret Hughes had to return again and again over a seven-week period to copy manually and compare visually for 3,120 employees what could have been done mechanically by one person in considerably less than 30 minutes for all city employees. The Civil Service Commission and the Mayor courteously complied with what they say is the letter of the law, but, in our opinion, they arbitrarily held back the full disclosure which the law really requires. Nevertheless the facts we learned, even under arduous conditions, are startling.

Summary of What We Found

1. In the ten departments we studied, we found striking discrimination against women employees, in terms of salary discrimination, concentration into low-paying clerical positions, and denial of advancement opportunities. Of the 3,120 city employees studied, 1,227 were full-time women employees.

61.36 percent of them were paid under $8,000. 80.8 percent of all full-time employees paid under $8,000 were women and 90.07 percent of all employees paid over $14,000 were men. The most flagrantly discriminatory department we found was the Law Department, where each appointment is solely in the discretion of the department head.

2. Most supervisory positions, by far, are held by men.

3. Most high-level positions are held by men, and are held under temporary appointments.

4. Temporary appointments serve as a means of effecting discrimination and also, through the TAs' increased likelihood of success in civil service examinations, of perpetuating it.

5. Although our study covered only 3,120 of about 35,000 city employees, we know in addition that for 4,000 firefighters and 13,000 policemen, the city prescribes that they be men. There are fewer than 100 police employees in the job title of "Policewoman." 1,507 lower-paid "Crossing Guards" are women.

6. In addition to our study, we know from the last budget debate (Council Journal 1593, December 11, 1971) that the city government has at least three job titles ("Janitress," "Maid," and "Scrubwoman") in which only women are employed and the wages are lower than for the equivalent job titles for men. The city administration has refused to change the titles or the pay.

7. In many positions held exclusively by persons of one sex, sex does not appear to be a bona fide occupational qualification. The segregation appears to rest on intention, traditions, or assumptions. Examples are "Environmental Sampling and Equipment Technicians," "Building Code Enforcement Inspectors," "Display Artists," "Computer Console Operators," and "Storekeepers," all of which are men.

8. Only three of the city's 41 departments are directed by women; namely, Consumer Sales with 67 employees, Municipal Reference Library with 14, and Alcoholic Treatment Center with 53, making a total of 134 employees, or *less than 1/2 of 1 percent of the city's 35,000 employees.*

9. The employment discrimination against women exists in addition to employment discrimination against Blacks. The Black woman is thus in an especially disfavored position in city employment. A similar observation applies to Latin Americans.

10. On employment discrimination against women, the city government has neither disclosed full information nor adopted any effective program to correct discrimination.

APPENDIX 5

The Despres Papers

After I retired from the City Council, my aldermanic and legal papers were deposited at the Chicago Historical Society. By great good fortune, the staff there followed up on my work and put the materials in shape to be of easy access and ready use by the people of Chicago, especially researchers and writers.

When I first became an alderman, I did not expect to be reelected. Quite the contrary. I thought that my passion for civil liberties, minority rights, and city planning would mark me for defeat. Even though I foresaw only a single four-year term, I decided to keep a complete record of outgoing correspondence to show what a Chicago alderman did in the twentieth century. In addition, inspired by the methods of my predecessor, Robert E. Merriam, my staff and I followed a fairly thorough classification of other aldermanic papers.

The four years grew to twenty. My records at the Chicago Historical Society now consist of 103 linear feet, 249 indexed boxes, and 22 reels of microfilm. Besides representing my twenty years as alderman, they also include some material on my years as lawyer, member of the Chicago Plan Commission, and parliamentarian of the Chicago City Council.

When I gave the records to CHS in 1975, we agreed on a ten-year stricture against access to preserve their current confidentiality. Apparently their completeness is exceptional. The late Archibald Motley Jr., the legendary and kind archivist of the Chicago Historical Society who supervised the papers' integration into the society's collections, spelled out their use and value in an interview with Kenan Heise:

> The Leon Despres papers represent one of the great political collections anyone has. What is extraordinary is their systematic organization covering such subjects as the City Council, civil rights, patronage, Mayor Daley, individual

aldermen, neighborhood life, censorship, gangs, reform, and Chicago politics.

This archive tells in detail the story of a man who was a major force for decency and civic responsibility and who routinely assisted minorities and other people who did not have much power in Chicago.

Our call slips show us that these records have been used by prominent authors writing about Chicago as well as by researchers interested in only one part of the overall picture.

Archives just do not have complete records from a twenty-year span of a politician's life and career. These are central to Chicago's political life and comprehensive on the issues that faced the city during two thirds of the twentieth century.

I am most appreciative of the efforts made in 1993 by Jay F. Clark and Gary Stockton at CHS, who inventoried the papers and created the usable forty-nine-page index and outline, which serves as a convenient guide to the papers.

Nothing was omitted. When my term ended and I was ready to give up the aldermanic office, we simply shipped everything to the Chicago Historical Society.

The society's three-page summary of the material contained in the Despres Papers follows.

DESCRIPTION OF THE PAPERS

The Leon M. Despres papers, 1945–1982 (mainly 1955–1975), consist primarily of subject files and correspondence generated during Despres' twenty years as Alderman of the Fifth Ward in Chicago. The papers relate primarily to Despres' political and social interests as alderman of the Hyde Park neighborhood but include some materials from his career as a lawyer.

The Despres papers are divided into three series: Aldermanic Records, 1947–1982; Fifth Ward Citizens' Committee, 1945–1975; and Legal Activities, 1947–1973.

Series I. Aldermanic Records, 1947–1982 (boxes 1–213, plus 22 reels of microfilm)

This first and largest series consists of records compiled from Despres' twenty-year career as Fifth Ward Alderman and comprises microfilm copies of newsclippings, copies of outgoing correspondence, telephone request and complaint cards from constituents, and subject files. The Aldermanic Records are divided into the following four subseries.

Subseries 1. Microfilm News Clippings, 1953–1982 (22 reels)

The microfilm copies of newsclippings were compiled and prepared by Despres' staff and are arranged chronologically. The newsclippings are primarily from Chicago and neighborhood newspapers and mostly concern Despres in both his aldermanic and legal careers. The microfilm also includes copies of announcements, programs, newsletters, and a few articles and speeches. This subseries provides the researcher with a good overview of Despres' career during this period and, consequently, a sampling of Chicago city politics at this time.

Subseries 2. Outgoing Correspondence, 1955–1975 (boxes 1–25)

Subseries 2 consists of chronologically arranged carbon copies of Despres' outgoing aldermanic correspondence. This group of material is extensive and concerns a wide variety of topics. Additional copies of a majority of these letters are also found in the topically-arranged subject files. (Subseries 4)

Subseries 3. Telephone Request and Complaint Cards, 1953–1975 (boxes 26–35)

These 3-inch-by-5-inch index cards are a record of the incoming telephone calls received by Alderman Despres' office from his constituents. The request and complaint cards are filed chronologically (and within each year are arranged alphabetically by name of constituent) and concern such matters as requests for installation of traffic signals and street lights, building code and traffic violations, employment requests, assistance with draft deferrals, neighborhood upkeep, and crime.

Subseries 4. Aldermanic Subject Files, 1947–1975 (boxes 36–213)

The Aldermanic Subject Files is the largest group of material in the collection and reflects the wide range of subjects that were of concern to Despres over the course of his aldermanic career. This material consists of such items as incoming correspondence and copies of outgoing correspondence, reports and studies, proposed legislation and resolution, and newsclippings. Topics and issues which the subject files address include city finances and planning, discrimination in housing and employment, pollution, public education,

crime, urban renewal, and zoning. Most of Subseries 4 is arranged alphabetically by subject heading (see container list), with the amount of the material
for each subject varying. The last four boxes of this subseries (210–213)
consist of additional aldermanic records which are of the same nature as the
rest of Subseries 4 but are filed chronologically, spanning 1948 to 1973.

Series II. Fifth Ward Citizens' Committee, 1945–1975 (boxes 214–240)

The Fifth Ward Citizens' Committee (FWCC) was "formed for charitable
and educational purposes within the Fifth Ward and throughout the city of
Chicago." The primary focus of the material in this series is the FWCC's
work with Alderman Despres, particularly its efforts to aid his election
campaigns in the form of fund drives and benefits, from 1955 to 1971. The
files also contain some records of the organization such as minutes, correspondence, and financial records. The series is divided into two subseries,
General Files and Financial Records.

Subseries 1. General Files (boxes 214–226)

Subseries 1 is the alphabetically arranged general files of the Fifth Ward
Citizens' Committee which include general correspondence, correspondence to and from contributors, and correspondence with Despres; press
releases and newsclippings; copies of leaflets, newsletters, and campaign lit-
erature; FWCC by-laws, meeting minutes, and some personnel files; and
information regarding fund drives and benefits. Much of the material under
any one subject heading overlaps with that in others. Furthermore, there is
additional material on campaigns and elections filed under the heading
"Elections" in Series 1, Subseries 4, Aldermanic Subject Files.

Subseries 2. Financial Records (boxes 227–240)

The FWCC financial records consist of receipts, cancelled checks, accounting
statements, and other similar material which detail the funds received and
distributed by the organization. The records are arranged chronologically.

Series III. Legal Activities, 1947–1973 (boxes 241–249)

Series III is comprised of a select group of records and papers which Despres
compiled as an attorney in private practice. They are divided into the following two subseries.

Subseries 1. American Civil Liberties Union (Illinois Division,
1947–1962 (boxes 241–244)

The small group of material in this subseries concerns Despres' activities
with the Illinois Division of the American Civil Liberties Union, and consists of correspondence, meeting minutes, newsclippings, and other related
papers. The items are arranged alphabetically by subject and include material on cases and issues concerning such topics as censorship, labor issues,
minority issues, and McCarthyism and loyalty statements.

Subseries 2. Leopold-Levin Litigation, 1958–1973 (boxes 245–249)

These papers consist of court records and attorney's files relative to Nathan
F. Leopold's law suit against Meyer Levin. Leopold and Richard Loeb,
University of Chicago students, were convicted in 1924 of the murder of 14
year old Bobby Franks in Chicago. Levin authored a novel and play entitled
Compulsion, based on the murder and ensuing trial, to which Leopold
objected on the basis of invasion of privacy. In addition to Levin, Leopold
named Simon and Schuster, the book's publisher, and 20th Century Fox, the
producer of a movie based on the book, as defendants. Despres successfully
served as co-counsel for these defendants. Specific materials in this collection include: plaintiff's exhibits and legal memos, an abstract of Leopold's
deposition, a transcript of proceedings, copies of the Circuit Court Judgment,
a record of the appeal, Illinois Supreme Court papers, correspondence,
newsclippings, and a copy of the book, *Compulsion*.

Index

Abrahamson, Julia, 15

Adamowski, Benjamin, 86, 106

Addams, Jane, xiii

Adler, Dankmar, 53

Adoption cases, 39

African Americans, 4, 13; acceptance of
LMD by, 85, 97–98; on CIO board, 84;
on city council, *see* Aldermen; color bar at
University of Chicago, 19, 25, 26; Daley's
relationship with, 45–46, 82–83, 88–89,
90, 95–98, 140, (patronage) 45, 85–86,
146–47, 148; Democratic Machine and,
85–86, 146, (as members) 107; employment discrimination against, (city
government) 152, (police and fire
departments) 95–96; Great Migration of,
136–37, 139; housing for, 69, 81–83, 86,
136–43, (Black Belt) 137–38, (Black
Metropolis) 136, 140, (homes bombed)
137–38; independent Senatorial
candidates, 149; LMD's contact with/
work for, 19, 81–89, 111, 145, (black
acceptance of) 85, 97–98; urban renewal
feared by, 66, 81, 143. *See also* Racism

Aldermen: black, 83, 84, 90, 92, 93, 147,
(Silent Six) 89, 146, 147, 148; conviction
and imprisonment of, 5, 45, 105, 107–9,
116; election campaigns, *see* Elections,
aldermanic; Jewish, 89; LMD as
alderman, *see* Despres, Leon M.: service
as alderman; Machine, 86, 111, 123;
payoffs, 104, (LMD's attack on) 36 (*see*

also Patronage system); salaries, 32, 35;
women as, 113–16. *See also* Chicago City
Council

Aldis, Graham, 49

Alinsky, Saul, xiii, 78, 80

*Alliance to End Repression and American Civil
Liberties Union v. City of Chicago*, 110

Alschuler, Alfred S., 58

Alschuler, Marian. *See* Despres, Mrs. Leon M.

American Civil Liberties Union (ACLU),
23; Illinois Division, 26, (LMD's papers
regarding) 157; sues City of Chicago, 110

American Dilemma (Myrdal), 142

American Historical Association, 95

American Institute of Architects, 50

American Pharaoh (Adams and Taylor), 38, 39

American Political Science Association, 113

Andelman, Dr. Samuel, 100, 103

Anderson, Douglas, 30

Another Country (Baldwin), 147

Architecture, preservation of, 47–57, 65

Arthur Cushman McGiffert House, 52

Art Institute, 50, 55, 56

Artman, Joseph, 9

Arvey, Jacob "Jack," 8, 71

Atwood, Sybil, 118

Austin community, 94

Bach, Ira, 56, 81

Balaban and Katz (theater owners), 53–54

Baldwin, James, 147

Bauler, Mathias "Paddy," 3, 58, 60

LEON M. DESPRES was born in 1908 in Chicago. He graduated from the University of Chicago Law School in 1929. Since leaving the Chicago City Council in 1975, he has served as a parliamentarian for the Jane Byrne and Harold Washington administrations and worked as an attorney, a teacher, and a lecturer. Despres lives in the Hyde Park neighborhood of Chicago.

KENAN HEISE spent seven years as a Franciscan monk before starting a thirty-year career at the *Chicago Tribune*. His many books include *Chicago the Beautiful: A City Reborn* and *Resurrection Mary: A Ghost Story*.